Odd Meter Bass
Complex Time Signatures Made Easy

Timothy Emmons

Stream or download the audio content for this book.
To access, visit: **alfred.com/redeem**
Enter the following code: 00-25578_994411

Alfred

alfred.com

ISBN-10: 0-7390-4081-2 (Book & Online Audio)
ISBN-13: 978-0-7390-4081-2 (Book & Online Audio)

Cover guitar photo courtesy of James Tyler Guitars.

Contents

Preface 3
  Acknowledgements 3
  Audio Production Credits. 3

Introduction. 4
  How This Book Works. 4
  The What, Where, When, Who, Why, and How of Odd-Meter Music 4

Chapter 1
It's As Easy As 1, 2, 3 6
  Time Signatures. 6
  Three Steps to Mastery. 6

Chapter 2
Not Odd Yet: Groups of Two or Four 11
  The Three Levels of Harmonic/Melodic Density 14
  The Magic Dotted Rhythms 15
  Applying the Three Steps to Mastery 17

Chapter 3
Getting Odder: Groups of Three 19
  Typical $\frac{3}{4}$ Styles. 21
  Sample $\frac{3}{4}$ Bass Lines 22
  Applying the Three Steps to Mastery 27

Chapter 4
Now This Is Odd: Groups of Five 31
  $\frac{5}{4}$ Meter 31
  $\frac{5}{8}$ Meter 37

Chapter 5
Seven and Seven Is: Groups of Seven 41

Chapter 6
Number Nine: Groups of Nine 49

Chapter 7
Die Elf: Groups of Eleven 57

Chapter 8
Really Odd: Groups of 13, 15, and More 65
  "Birds of Fire" 66

Chapter 9
Mixed-Meter Music 73

Chapter 10
The Songs (Basically Remain the Same) 80

Bibliography and Discography 86

About the Author 88

Preface

There are many books elucidating odd-meter performance for drummers. Until recently, players of other instruments have had to adapt that material on their own. This book is a specific application of these proven drum techniques to the bass. You can also use this material with the other rhythm section instruments. I know from personal experience that this approach really works. I hope you'll enjoy this book and your journey to understanding and mastering odd-meter music.

Tim Emmons

Acknowledgements

I would like to thank drummer and author Ed Roscetti, who first encouraged me to do the book in 2003 and from whom I first learned the drummer's approach to odd-meter music; Aaron Stang at Alfred Music for his patience and continued commitment to the project, and Kate Westin at Alfred Music for putting the pieces together into a real book; Mike Packer of Freeflight for playing the perfect drum parts; Bryan Pezzone of Freeflight for the use of his composition "Methane 5," and Jim Walker of Freeflight for hiring me in 2000 and giving me the opportunity to play with his legendary odd-meter band; Kenton Youngstrom for playing so well and recording the audio over a protracted production schedule; James Tyler of Tyler Guitars for building a wonderful instrument; Mike Tempesta of Yamaha Guitars for the TRB1006 and Ken Smith for the strings; all the master musicians and recording artists who influenced the material in this book.

Special thanks to my loving wife, Leslie Emmons, for typing the text and for her unwavering support and encouragement, and to my son, Alexander, who reminds me to keep it light.

Audio Production Credits

Produced by Timothy Emmons and Kenton Youngstrom
Recorded at Major Label Studios, South Pasadena, CA
Tracks written by Timothy Emmons
Electric and acoustic basses: Timothy Emmons
Electric and acoustic guitars: Kenton Youngstrom
Drums: Michael Packer

 Use audio Track 1 to tune your bass.

Introduction

How This Book Works

The purpose of this book is to help bassists decipher the mysterious language of *odd-meter* rhythm. Once a musician comprehends the concept of reducing complex meters into simple odd and even groupings, the inherent structure of odd-meter music will be revealed. When a player feels secure rhythmically, he or she can relax and perform and improvise with confidence.

I must confess that I, initially, had a terrible time trying to play odd-meter music. Then, a drummer taught me the subdivision concept, and I finally saw the way to decipher odd-meter (and "regular-meter") rhythmic problems. At last, I had found a consistently effective procedure to interpret any rhythmic figure!

Realizing that complex rhythms can be subdivided into small, manageable rhythmic groupings is the key to unlocking the secret of odd-meter music. The work it takes to learn odd meters also deepens one's understanding of "normal" music such as that in $\frac{4}{4}$ and $\frac{3}{4}$.

I want to show bassists how to use this approach. **It always works!**

The What, Where, When, Who, Why, and How of Odd-Meter Music

What is an "odd meter"? What we call *odd-meter music* is what musicologists refer to as *compound additive meter* or *asymmetric meter*. A complete definition would begin with the idea of music organized in repeating rhythmic groups of three, five, seven, nine, eleven, thirteen, fifteen, etc. The definition could continue to mention the emotional quality that an unusual rhythm may impart.

Odd-meter music is only "odd" because most of us haven't heard much of it. Musicians who limit their listening to Western music (of European origin) will be most familiar with rhythmic groupings of two, three, or four. Most rock and popular contemporary music is organized in $\frac{4}{4}$ meter.

Rhythms in $\frac{2}{4}$ and $\frac{2}{2}$ are very common in marches and Broadway musical theater compositions. The $\frac{3}{4}$ rhythms include the waltz and the Spanish bolero. A $\frac{9}{8}$ rhythm can be played as three groups of three pulses, and $\frac{6}{8}$ rhythm is commonly played as two groups of three; it all depends on how we subdivide and group the smallest common rhythmic denominator. The overarching "two" or "three" feel is the result of how you group the smaller rhythmic subdivisions.

Where did odd-meter music come from? The Balkans, Greece, and Asia Minor spawned indigenous music with odd rhythmic groupings. The music of India is performed in complex odd-meter units. I have seen Balkan and South Indian dances choreographed to these odd-meter phrases. If you watch a troop of Balkan folk dancers, you will see the odd meter accommodated with special steps. Music that developed in West Africa is complexly polyrhythmic with fairly simple melodic lines and little or no use of harmonic elements. Indian classical music utilizes complex rhythmic and melodic elements with a much more static harmonic environment than European music.

Across the globe and throughout history, most musical expression has been rhythmic and melodic in nature. Harmony came into use as an important element in Europe only in the last half-millennium or so. In most societies, people traditionally sing or play individual melodic lines, and the rhythmic accompaniment energizes the lyrical content and the performance. Rhythm aids in memorization, induces trances, and eases shared work.

When did odd-meter music develop? As mentioned earlier, many cultures use what we may call "odd meters" in their folk music. The origins are ancient—certainly thousands of years old. Recently, a tentative date was established for the origin of human musical expression with the discovery of a Neolithic ivory flute in a European cave site dated circa 30,000 BCE. Dozens of still-playable bird-bone flutes, dated circa 9000 BCE, were recently discovered in China. The scales on the flutes ranged from five to eight tones, and some were quite close to our contemporary major scale.

The history of European music offers a few examples of compound additive-meter composition. A few examples of quintuple-meter passages date from as early as the 14th century. Apparently, the first surviving deliberate quintuple-meter compositions were published in Spain between 1516 and 1520. An early use of $\frac{5}{8}$ meter for dramatic effect is found in Handel's *Orlando* (1732). By the 19th century, European composers began to purposefully use odd meters in their works. Wagner's *Tristan and Isolde* (1859) employs an example of $\frac{5}{4}$ to underscore a traumatic dramatic event in the opera. The second movement of Tchaikovsky's *Symphony No. 6, "Pathetique"* (1893), is a pseudo-waltz written in $\frac{5}{4}$ time signature.

Who writes odd-meter music? Composers writing for ballet and theater were among the first to use asymmetrical additive meters purposefully. In 1913, Igor Stravinsky engendered a firestorm of musical opprobrium by using mixed and odd meters in his score for the ballet *The Rite of Spring*. The Paris premiere of the work shattered audience expectations with its innovative use of primitive-sounding odd-meter rhythms, and the audience's raucous reaction mirrored the pagan dancers' performance on stage. Late 19th-century Russian composer Alexander Borodin evoked the savage energy of Slavic folk music by using mixed $\frac{2}{4}$ and $\frac{3}{4}$ meters in his *Symphony No. 2 in B Minor*. Béla Bartók's collection of piano pieces titled *Mikrocosmos* includes numerous compositions in odd meters inspired by his research of the folk music of his native Hungary.

Why write music in odd meters? For the emotional effect! Gustav Holst wrote the "Mars" theme from *The Planets* in $\frac{5}{4}$ to underscore the innate brutality of war. Holst's merciless juggernaut ominously advances to a sinister $\frac{5}{4}$ cadence. Leonard Bernstein used odd meters to depict the spastic energy of the inhabitants of the modern urban jungle in *West Side Story*. Samuel Barber used asymmetrical groupings of eight notes over the bar line in mixed $\frac{5}{8}$ and $\frac{6}{8}$ meters to create a tumbling cascade of arpeggios in his *Tocatta Festival Concerto for Organ and Orchestra*. Fusion guitarist John McLaughlin achieved the same effect with a quintet and lots of big amplifiers.

As a session and show player, I frequently encounter odd meters in film, television, theater music, and commercials. Besides the obvious emotional effect created by an odd meter, a composer may use odd-meter bars to catch the action in a chase scene or support a particular visual element.

Composition to accompany modern dance is rife with odd and mixed meters. *Appalachian Spring*, written by Aaron Copland for Martha Graham's dance company, is an excellent example from the 1940s. Contemporary musical theater composers use odd meters for dramatic effect. The musicals *Jesus Christ Superstar* by Andrew Lloyd Webber, *Pippin* by Steven Schwartz, and *Aida* by Elton John all contain excellent examples. Contemporary rock bands such as Tool, Rush, and Dream Theater use odd meters extensively.

How do I get some of this odd-meter stuff? Easy: **Use this book now!**

In the first three chapters, we will explore the subdivision concept and apply it to some familiar meters before moving on to odd meters. You will learn a basic three-step procedure to master the specific rhythm of choice and compose bass lines and solos from chords and scales. We will work with the subdivision concept in "two" meters and "three" meters first and inculcate a technique for approaching odd rhythmic groupings.

From chapter 4 on, things will get really odd as we work on successive odd meters. Eventually, we will mix up various odd and even meters. The secret formula is my patented three-step process of mastery for solving rhythmic and melodic problems in any meter or style. **It always works!**

Chapter 1
It's As Easy As 1, 2, 3

The basic premise of this book is that you can subdivide intricate rhythms into familiar pieces by thinking and feeling small rhythmic groups. These short rhythmic units can be grouped together in various combinations to comprise more complex rhythmic phrases. Simply find the smallest common rhythmic denominator of any given meter and subdivide the rhythmically challenging figures into easy-to-manage groups of one, two, or three notes. Larger combinations of beats can be felt as compounds of these smaller groupings. Drummers think this way all the time, and this concept is the secret to understanding any rhythm in any meter.

Rhythm is the motor that propels a musical performance. Its pulse sets the stage for the action of the other main characters in music: melody and harmony. Teaching you to feel the pulse of a piece of music and organize apparently complex pulses into simpler groupings at will is the goal of this book. Becoming comfortable rhythmically in any meter is a prerequisite to playing a great bass line.

In order to master the rhythms, you will be doing some rhythmic exercises with your hands before ever touching the bass. You can, and should, work on the rhythmic figures out of time, but **always use a metronome** when you practice at tempo. "Rhythmic feel" is a nebulous concept because "feel" is so subjective—you know it when you hear it. Nonetheless, we strive to move the listener emotionally with the rhythmic impulse we create. Ultimately, as bassists, our "feel" is more important than the pitches we play.

Time Signatures

Before we start exploring odd meters, let's briefly review time signatures. The time element of music is represented by a symbol called a *time signature*, found in the staff after the clef and key signature before the first note. It resembles a fraction with one number over another. The top number tells the player how many *beats* (rhythmic pulses) will be contained in each repeating group called a *measure*. Measures are indicated in music notation by vertical lines in the staff called *bar lines*. The lower number in the time signature tells the player what type of note represents one beat, e.g., a quarter note.

The $\frac{4}{4}$ time signature means the rhythmic pulse is felt in groups of four, with each pulse denoted as a quarter note. The $\frac{5}{4}$ meter contains five quarter notes per measure. Music in $\frac{3}{4}$ time signatures is felt as bunches of three quarter notes. In all of these cases, the quarter note defines the rhythmic pulse. In a performance, we will almost certainly play notes that are longer or shorter in duration than a quarter note, but the quarter note remains the reference for the basic pulse.

The reason music is notated in different meters is to communicate the rhythmic feel of a piece. A fast march is easier to read and feel in $\frac{2}{2}$ where the melodic rhythms are usually written in eighth notes, quarter notes, and half notes. Slow funk music is usually written with sixteenth-note figures. It's all about best representing the actual feel of the music in a visible form of music notation.

In order to maintain an even tempo and play very accurately, we can also feel the basic pulse in shorter rhythmic units. We could think in eighth notes, sixteenth notes, triplets, etc., against the basic pulse of quarter notes. The smallest, shortest rhythmic unit in a piece will be its **smallest common denominator,** as any larger rhythmic figure in the piece will be divisible by it.

Three Steps to Mastery

Any rhythmic, melodic, or harmonic puzzle can be solved with the following routine.

Step 1: Do the Math

Research and familiarize yourself with the rhythmic phrase you want to master by subdividing it into smaller rhythmic groups. Then you can accent the first beat of whatever various groupings of one, two, or three occur within the overall rhythmic figure. The accented notes will be felt as syncopation against the basic pulse. These accented notes will then become the basis for the melodic rhythm of your bass line. Once you know what you are going to play rhythmically, then you can practice how to play it.

Step 2: Learn the Chords

Research the pitches you want to play out of tempo so that you know where you're going to physically find the notes on the fingerboard. Remember, the same note may be played on various strings at different frets. The position of any note is affected by the placement of the preceding note and your preparation for the following notes. Some licks lay out on the fingerboard better in one position than another.

What if there are no chords, per se? What if the music you play is strictly melodic and rhythmic without any chords? That's okay. Regardless of the style, you must familiarize yourself with the harmonic and/or melodic material you are going to play. The process of choosing the ideal location on the fingerboard sets the stage for applying your newly mastered odd-meter rhythms in tempo.

Step 3: Put It Together

Create your bass lines and/or solos. A bass line typically employs rhythmic figures with more repetition than those of a melody or solo. Bass figures will usually be built on the longer melodic rhythms created by sustaining the accented subdivisions of the meter. Drummers may orchestrate busier figures around the drumset because they deal with rhythms only. Bass lines tend to be rhythmically simpler—not that bass players don't sometimes play busy figures. The bass part should support the subdivision groupings. We will work on matching notes to rhythms in subsequent chapters.

The "Three Steps to Mastery" idea isn't just for bassists. This didactic technique applies to any meter and any instrument. Each time you work out an odd-meter time signature, use this procedure. This way, you will have a consistent approach to mastering any rhythmic situation. Follow the three steps, and you will always succeed in overcoming rhythmic challenges.

The physical act of practice is essential at this stage. **Do** practice slowly and correctly now, and it will be easy to work the figures up to speed in a relatively short period of time. **Do not** practice mistakes by playing too fast and sloppy at this stage. Yes, I know you want to play it fast like the recording, but you can't just erase a mistake you practiced into your muscle memory. You will have to take even more time to write a new set of instructions in your brain to override the mistake. Remember: garbage in, garbage out. First work out the figures without a click, then use a metronome or drum machine once you are ready to practice in tempo.

First, find the lowest common denominator for the rhythmic figures in question. For example, a phrase in $\frac{5}{4}$ meter will probably contain a rhythm figure involving eighth notes. So, when I work on the figures, I might use an eighth-note click on the metronome so that I can hear the smallest rhythmic unit involved in the figure. If the rhythms involve sixteenth notes, I will use a sixteenth-note click. A drum machine is also a great tool to use when working on odd-meter rhythms.

Once you have reduced the figures to their lowest common denominator, you can then organize them into groups of one, two, or three notes. Larger rhythmic groupings, such as dotted-quarter or half notes, will be combinations of these smaller rhythmic units that are the lower common denominators.

Always work out the rhythms before applying them to any bass line. Tap the rhythmic figures out on your legs or chest. If that's too painful, use a tabletop or clap them out. You *need* to do this physical process to get the rhythm out of your head and into your body. Feel the basic pulse in your feet while you play all the subdivisions with your hands and sing the accents. Applying the rhythms to the harmonic and melodic elements of your composition will create the bass lines.

Let's try applying this concept to a couple of real live odd-meter rhythms. Let's look at $\frac{5}{4}$ meter written with five quarter notes (example 1.1). You cannot divide the odd-numbered five-quarter-note rhythmic cell into two equal halves until you begin to think in eighth notes. Beat 3 has to be divided in half to find the middle of the measure (example 1.2).

Example 1.1

Example 1.2

In $\frac{5}{4}$ meter, you want to think in an eighth-note phrase that could be divided evenly. Example 1.3 ties the quarter notes together, and example 1.4 shows the same rhythm written with half notes tied to eighth notes—both examples are played exactly the same, but are notated differently.

Example 1.3

Example 1.4

To divide a $\frac{5}{4}$ measure into four rhythmically equal parts, you would think in sixteenth notes, as in example 1.5. The upper stave groups the sixteenth notes with a phrase marking against the quarter-note pulse. In the lower stave, grouping five sixteenth notes together creates the same phrasing. The first notation is visually clearer, but the second notation reflects what you will actually feel when you play this subdivision.

Example 1.5

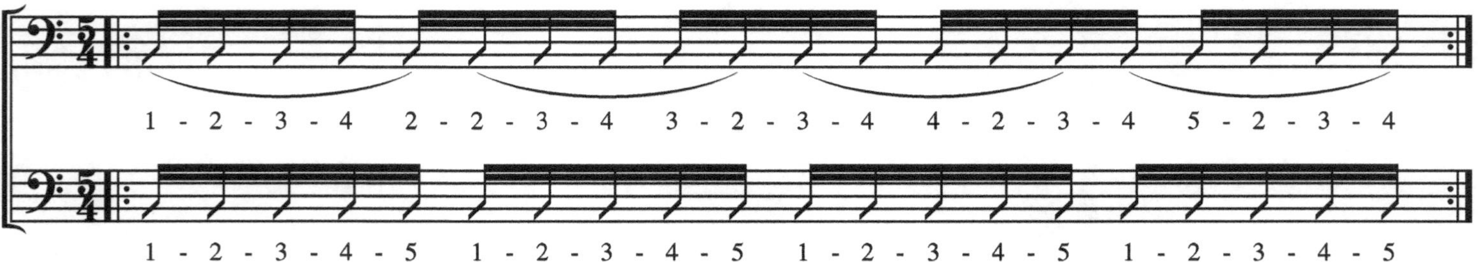

Now that I'm thinking in groups of sixteenths, I'm getting lost counting to five, so I'm going to group the 20 sixteenth notes into four 3+2 units. The groups of three and two sixteenths can be represented as a dotted eighth note and an eighth note (see example 1.6). These composite rhythms are shown in the lower staves of examples 1.6 through 1.9.

Example 1.6

Example 1.7 shows how you could also view the five sixteenths as 2+3 units, represented as an eighth note and a dotted eighth note. Either way, you have one odd and one even grouping that gives you some aural reference to delineate the beginning of the measure.

Example 1.7

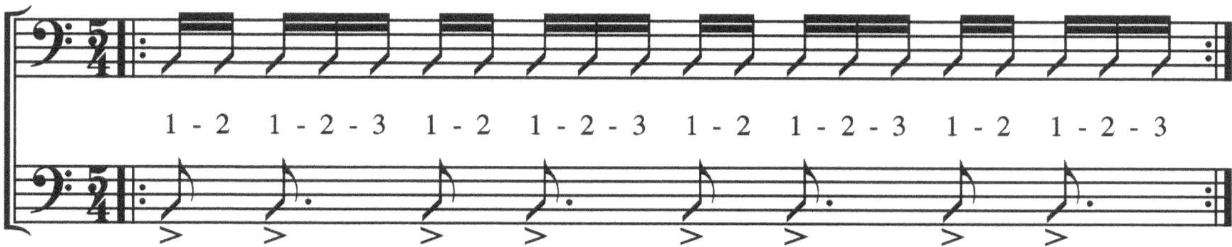

We could also mix the subdivisions at will, as shown in examples 1.8 and 1.9. When you actually compose bass lines, you will probably end up doing this to create a signature figure, a contrasting rhythmically unique fill, or a turnaround lick. The longer-value composite rhythm created by the accented notes at the beginning of each subdivision of two or three sixteenths will be the likely rhythms for many of my bass lines.

Example 1.8

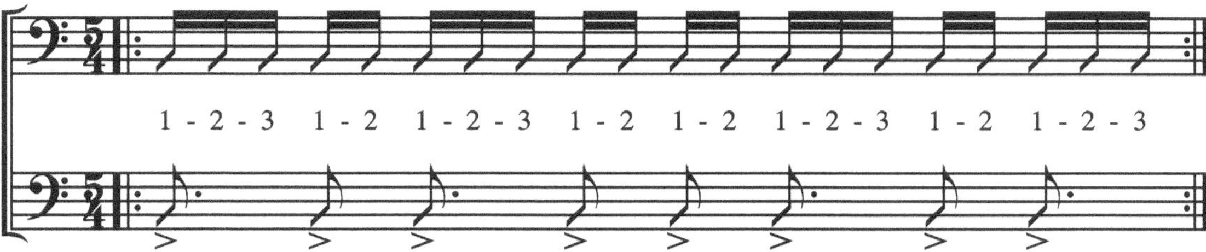

Example 1.9

In practice, you will often find that an odd-meter rhythm is primarily a "three" feel with odd groups of two. Example 1.10 shows how $\frac{11}{8}$ meter could be felt as three groups of three and one group of two.

Example 1.10

Compare the notation of example 1.10 with that of example 1.11. Example 1.11 shows the same $\frac{11}{8}$ meter subdivided as four groups of two with an odd three grouping. The accents created by these contrasting subdivisions will create two very different rhythmic feels, even though they are both written in $\frac{11}{8}$ meter.

Example 1.11

The two odd meters we have just examined will be further explored in later chapters. The idea here is to learn a problem-solving procedure and apply it consistently to each meter we study.

Once you have done your research on the rhythms and the notes you will play, you can put the two together and create your bass line or solo. To create a great bass line, you will want to have a balance between repetition and variation. Too much repetition is boring, and too much variation sounds like a solo. Also, don't forget that you are the harmonic foundation of the band, so note choice is important. The style of the music and the nature of each piece should determine what you play.

When I transcribe an odd-meter bass line, I use this process. Once I understand the rhythmic character of the piece, the pitches are much easier to learn. Keep in mind that if you cannot play the rhythms alone without the bass, you certainly will not be able to play them with the instrument. The compositional aspect of this method will be fully applied to each specific rhythm in subsequent chapters. Now that you have learned the Three Steps to Mastery, we can begin working with subdivisions in a familiar meter: $\frac{4}{4}$!

Chapter 2
Not Odd Yet: Groups of Two or Four

First, we are going to apply the subdivision technique in familiar rhythmic territory, $\frac{4}{4}$ meter. We are going to use the subdivision concept to decipher some standard syncopated rhythmic figures. You will find that, by thinking subdivisions in an even meter, you can create polyrhythmic effects within the measure, or odd-sounding phrases over the bar line. This rhythmic device is called a *hemiola*. Drummers think of this, I hope, when they play fills or setup figures. Bassists need to choose which pitches to play with these rhythms, so we will also do some bass line composition in this chapter.

Let's review the basic meter and potential smaller-denominator rhythms. Example 2.1 is a "rhythm pyramid" for $\frac{4}{4}$ meter. Each subsequent line in the example is a subdivision of the rhythm preceding it. I have included triplet figures in the pyramid, but in this book we will be working mainly with eighths and sixteenths.

Set your metronome anywhere from 60–100 beats per minute (bpm), and tap or clap the rhythms in example 2.1. Start slowly and accurately before increasing the tempo. If necessary, work out the figures without a click and *then* practice at tempo. By the time you get to the thirty-second notes in the last stave, you have played just about every probable rhythm in a bass line at 100 bpm. Any quicker rhythmic figures will start to sound like tremolos.

Example 2.1: Rhythm Pyramid for $\frac{4}{4}$

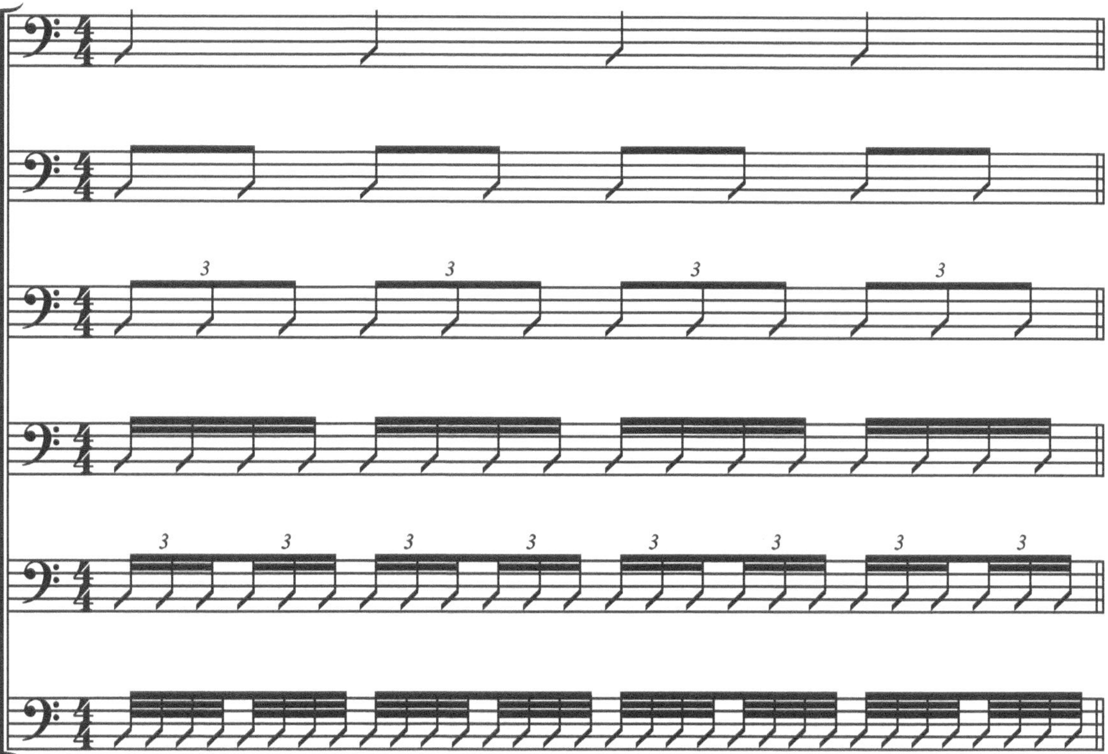

Now take a look at six common syncopated rhythms in $\frac{4}{4}$ meter (example 2.2). The first measure shows the standard rhythmic notation. The second measure is written to reflect the subdivisions of eighth notes into groups of one, two, or three. You are already subdividing when you read these familiar syncopated rhythms.

Two-measure bass lines are melodically interesting and provide a balance between repetition and variation. Your favorite bass player undoubtedly uses this concept. You could construct 36 rhythmically different two-measure phrases from the six figures in example 2.2.

Example 2.2

It's time to do the math on sixteenth-note subdivisions. Example 2.3 contains some common sixteenth-note rhythms and is organized the same way as the eighth-note subdivisions in example 2.2. Obviously, many more rhythmic options exist at the sixteenth-note level of lowest common denominator. The first measure of each line is written in standard rhythmic notation. The second measure shows the subdivision of that rhythm into groups of one, two, and three, based on the lowest common rhythmic denominator.

Example 2.3

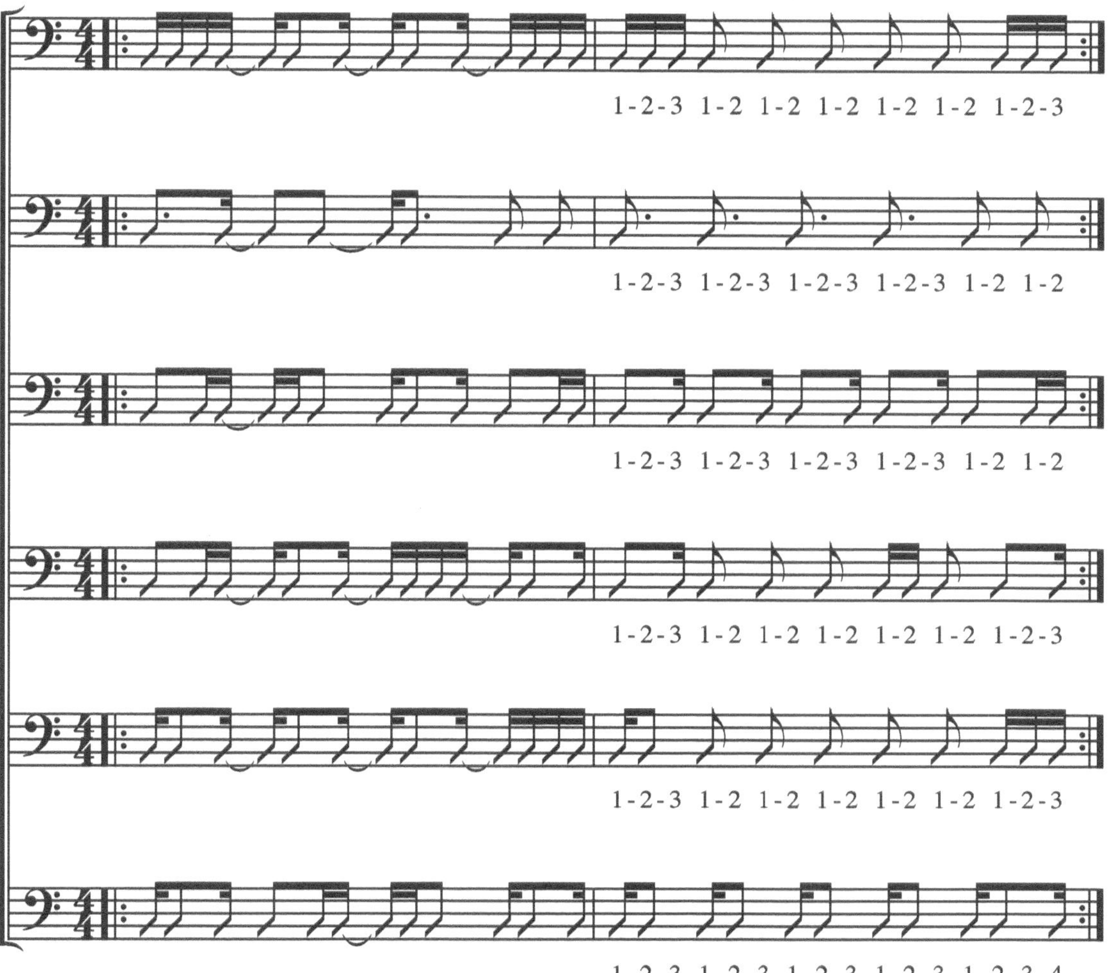

When you work out the rhythms of the subdivision groups, verbally accent the downbeat of each grouping. The first line of example 2.3 would be sung as ONE-two-three, ONE-two, ONE-two, ONE-two, ONE-two, ONE-two, ONE-two-three. As you sing the smallest rhythmic common denominator, clap or tap the largest composite rhythm. In the first line of example 2.3, this is a dotted eighth note, then five eighths, and then a dotted eighth note in each measure. I would create my bass line primarily from the larger composite rhythms.

The Three Levels of Harmonic/Melodic Density

I promised some compositional work, so let's take a break from the mathematics of rhythm and decide what pitches to play. As mentioned in chapter 1, you might play music that only uses melodic riffs and rhythmic figures, or the compositions could feature dense harmonic structures and unusual scales. No matter which part of the harmonic spectrum your music occupies, you will always have to make pitch choices based on the three options presented below in example 2.4.

Example 2.4

Level 1: Chordal (4 of 12)

If you play at this level, you will only be using chord tones in your bass line. The term "4 of 12" means that out of the 12 possible chromatic pitches, you select from the four tones of a seventh chord. This would create strongly harmonic bass lines with little melodic color. Of course, these bass lines would be harmonic in character, as they only use the chord tones, after all. This level of playing would include the last measure in level one of example 2.4; chugging eighth notes on the root is a staple of rock bass playing. Most bass lines, however, will use more than just the chord tones.

Level 2: Scalar (7 of 12)

At this level, you will incorporate notes from the appropriate scales for the chords. Since chord tones are just selected from a given scale, the use of scalar bass lines supports the harmony while adding melodic interest. Most bass figures we hear are at this level of density. The term "7 of 12" means that we are actually using just over half of the 12 possible chromatic tones in our bass line, since most scales have seven different pitches.

Level 3: Chromatic (12 of 12)

At this level, you will incorporate any one of the 12 chromatic pitches as approach notes to scale or chord tones. The excessive use of chromatic notes in a bass line tends to blur the harmonic function of the bass. I use chromatic tones sparingly in bass lines. Chromatic tones function best when they lead into a strong consonance. If you are soloing, you are free to try anything the band (and your audience) will accept; if you're creating a bass line, strongly consonant chord and scale tones are usually preferable.

The Magic Dotted Rhythms

We can produce an odd-meter feel in an even meter. It is time to check out subdivisions that result in "over-the-bar line" syncopations. As previously mentioned, a hemiola is created by simultaneously superimposing one rhythmic grouping over another. The effect is *polyrhythmic*: two different metric groupings being played at the same time. These figures will often play over the bar line. To help us out with these figures, let's meet my rhythm buddies, the magic dotted quarter and dotted eighth notes.

This concept is magical because feeling the dotted rhythm as one unit makes odd meter seem more "even." You can't play in the groove if you don't feel it in your body. You can tap your foot to "Take Five" with four taps if you feel the pulse as two dotted quarters and two quarters.

Playing groups of dotted eighths or sixteenths against an even eighth or sixteenth pulse quickly and easily creates interesting syncopations. A two-measure, or longer, phrase is a situation in which this effect can really be developed. Excellent rhythmic tension results from the collision of two superimposed metric units. For example, the bass could play dotted subdivisions against a straight four drumbeat, or a long phrase of an odd-numbered amount of notes will turn the beat around relative to the drum pattern. Led Zeppelin used the latter device in "Black Dog."

The next several examples have the standard notation in the top stave and the subdivision notation in the lower stave. The subdivision notation shows the same rhythmic durations with far fewer ties. Ties can be visually obscure. Read the upper notation and think the lower. Example 2.5 shows a two-measure 16-eighth-note phrase grouped 3+3+3+3+2+2. You get four dotted quarters and two even quarters at the end of the two-measure phrase. You can hear this type of syncopation in "String of Pearls" by Glenn Miller (circa 1940) and "Kashmir" by Led Zeppelin (circa 1974).

Example 2.5

Example 2.6 shows how the dotted quarter-note subdivision from example 2.5 would appear if the figure starts with an odd rest of one eighth at the beginning of the first measure. This syncopation is more driving, creating a sort of "5-over-8" effect. You can hear this rhythmic idea used over a four-measure phrase in "Jungle Boogie" by Kool & the Gang.

Example 2.6

Example 2.7 shows how this idea could be spun out over a four-bar phrase in $\frac{4}{4}$. You could play 10 dotted quarters over a four-measure phrase as 10 groups of three eighths (10 x 3 = 30 eighths), with the last two eighth notes at the end of the phrase.

Example 2.7

Example 2.8 shows the first of three possible groupings of sixteenths using the magic dotted rhythm concept. The composite rhythm of 10 dotted eighths and an even eighth note is shown in the lower stave. The shortest note is at the end of the phrase.

Example 2.8

Example 2.9 shows the opposite type of subdivision as shown in example 2.8. This example is similar to example 2.6 in that the short rhythm is at the beginning of the phrase.

Example 2.9

Example 2.10 has the same rhythmic effect as example 2.7, except that it is notated in sixteenth notes. The tempo would be slower in a sixteenth-note groove, so the rhythmic effect of the two examples would be quite similar.

Example 2.10

Applying the Three Steps to Mastery

We'll finish this chapter by applying the Three Steps to Mastery to some real musical situations. Let's stay in $\frac{4}{4}$ meter but create syncopation over the bar line using the magic dotted quarter note. Use the 3+3+3+3+2+2 subdivision of eighth notes from example 2.5.

1. Do the Math: Play the rhythmic subdivision of the larger rhythms, the quarters and dotted quarters, on your body while singing the accents of the subdivision groupings. For example, tap out a steady eighth-note rhythm on your thighs while you sing the longer duration quarter and dotted quarter notes. Use a hard syllable like "TA" for rhythmic clarity. Doing this rhythm practice on the body is essential.

Once you master the rhythmic figures, practice using the metronome for tempo reference. Start at a tempo where you can play all the material without mistakes, and then gradually increase the tempo. This process actually takes less time than attempting to play fast right away.

2. Learn the Chords: We have decided to use an E7 harmonic structure and an E Mixolydian scale. Find the pitch locations on the fingerboard, and practice the scales and arpeggios in different positions with alternate fingerings. Always use the metronome when practicing technical material at tempo.

3. Put It Together: We decide on a rhythmic feel such as funk sixteenths or samba in cut time. The choice of rhythmic style will determine the kinds of bass lines we compose. Then, we put it together, and we could have a bass line like the one in example 2.11.

Example 2.11  Track 2

Let's repeat this compositional process with the subdivision from example 2.6. If we use the same harmonic and melodic material, the result could be the lick shown below in example 2.12. The fundamental bass figure is built around the larger common composite groupings of quarters and dotted quarter notes.

The end of the second and fourth measures have melodic fills leading to the next primary harmonic downbeats in measures 1 and 3. Drummers do this sort of setup figure all the time. Bassists can add a melodic element at these important spots in the phrase.

Example 2.12  Track 3

One more example in $\frac{4}{4}$ and then we'll move on to groups of three. Example 2.13 is a marriage of the sixteenth-note rhythm from example 2.10 and the E blues scale. In the first two measures, you will see the standard notation for this rhythmic figure. In the next two measures, the figure is written to show the groupings of three sixteenths using the magic dotted eighth-note rhythm.

Example 2.13 Track 4

The subdivision notation in measures 3 and 4 reflects the way we actually hear and feel the melodic rhythm of the bass line; however, it's hard to read because it visually obscures the middle of the measure. By now you should be getting familiar with the practice of viewing syncopations as subdivisions. Let's go on to chapter 3 and do some work with rhythms based on groups of three.

Chapter 3
Getting Odder: Groups of Three

In this chapter, we will work with music notated in groups of three. This could include $\frac{3}{4}$, $\frac{3}{8}$, $\frac{3}{16}$, and $\frac{3}{2}$ meters. Later we will encounter some meters that use compound groups of three, such as $\frac{6}{8}$, $\frac{9}{8}$, and $\frac{15}{8}$. While three *is* an odd number, the "three" feel of a waltz is very familiar to most people. Music based in three is common to many cultures around the world. Our work on meters in three will give us another chance to master the subdivision concept in a familiar rhythmic environment.

Let's look at our rhythm pyramid for $\frac{3}{4}$. Set your metronome, and tap or clap the rhythms in example 3.1. Set a tempo no faster than that at which you can play *all* the rhythms correctly *before* increasing the tempo. DO practice perfection. DO NOT practice mistakes. By the time you get to the thirty-second notes in stave six, you will have played almost any rhythm probable in a bass line at 100 bpm. We will be primarily interested in larger rhythmic values for our bass lines anyway.

Example 3.1: Rhythm Pyramid for $\frac{3}{4}$

Look at example 3.2. We have grouped the eighth-note subdivision of $\frac{8}{4}$ into various combinations of one, two, or three eighth notes. The first measure of each line is written with ties and the second measure is written without ties to show the groupings. Set your metronome and tap or clap the rhythmic variations.

Example 3.2

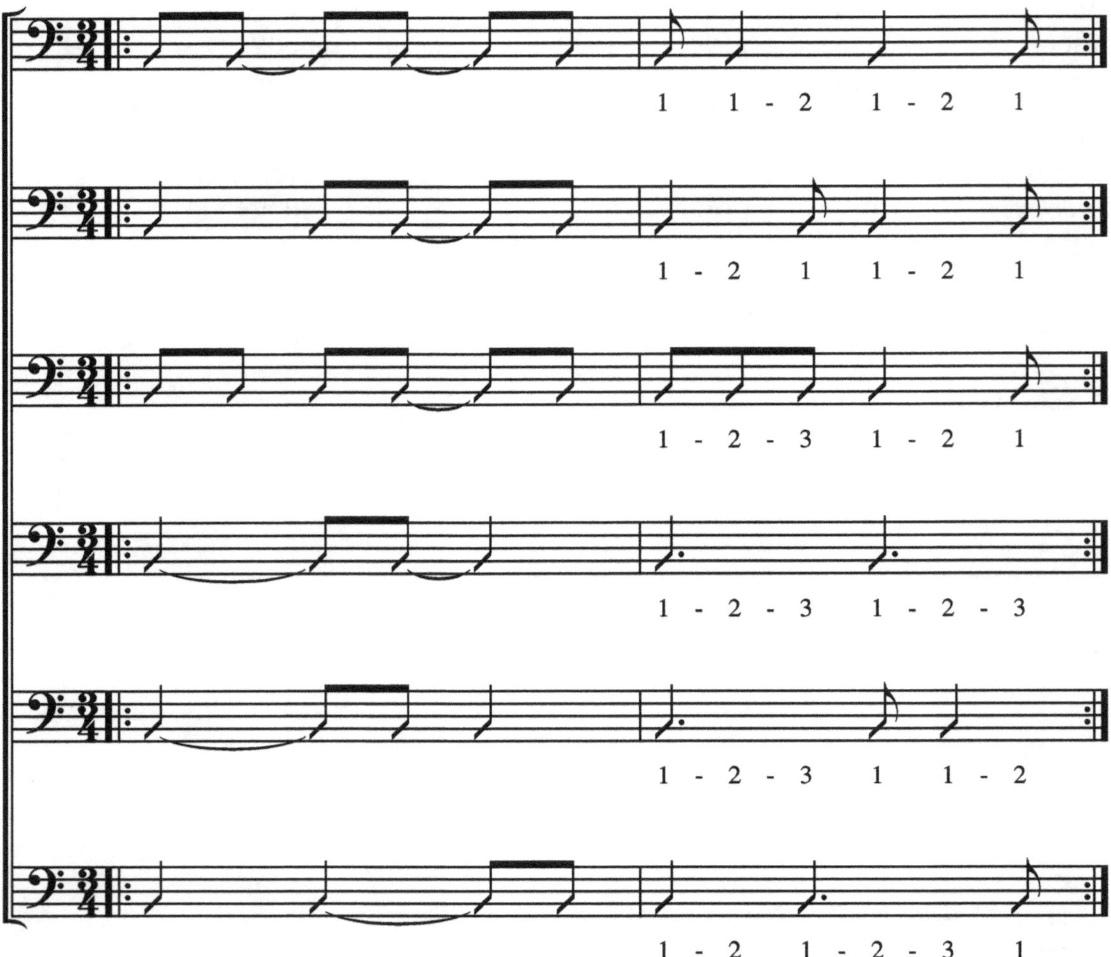

Now let's create some smaller rhythmic subdivisions by using combinations of sixteenth notes. Set the metronome, slowly at first, and tap or clap the rhythmic variations in example 3.3. The first four figures are driving and syncopated. The last two have a loping "four-over-three" feel. The first measure of each line is written with ties, and the second measure is written without ties to show the groups of two or three sixteenth notes.

Example 3.3

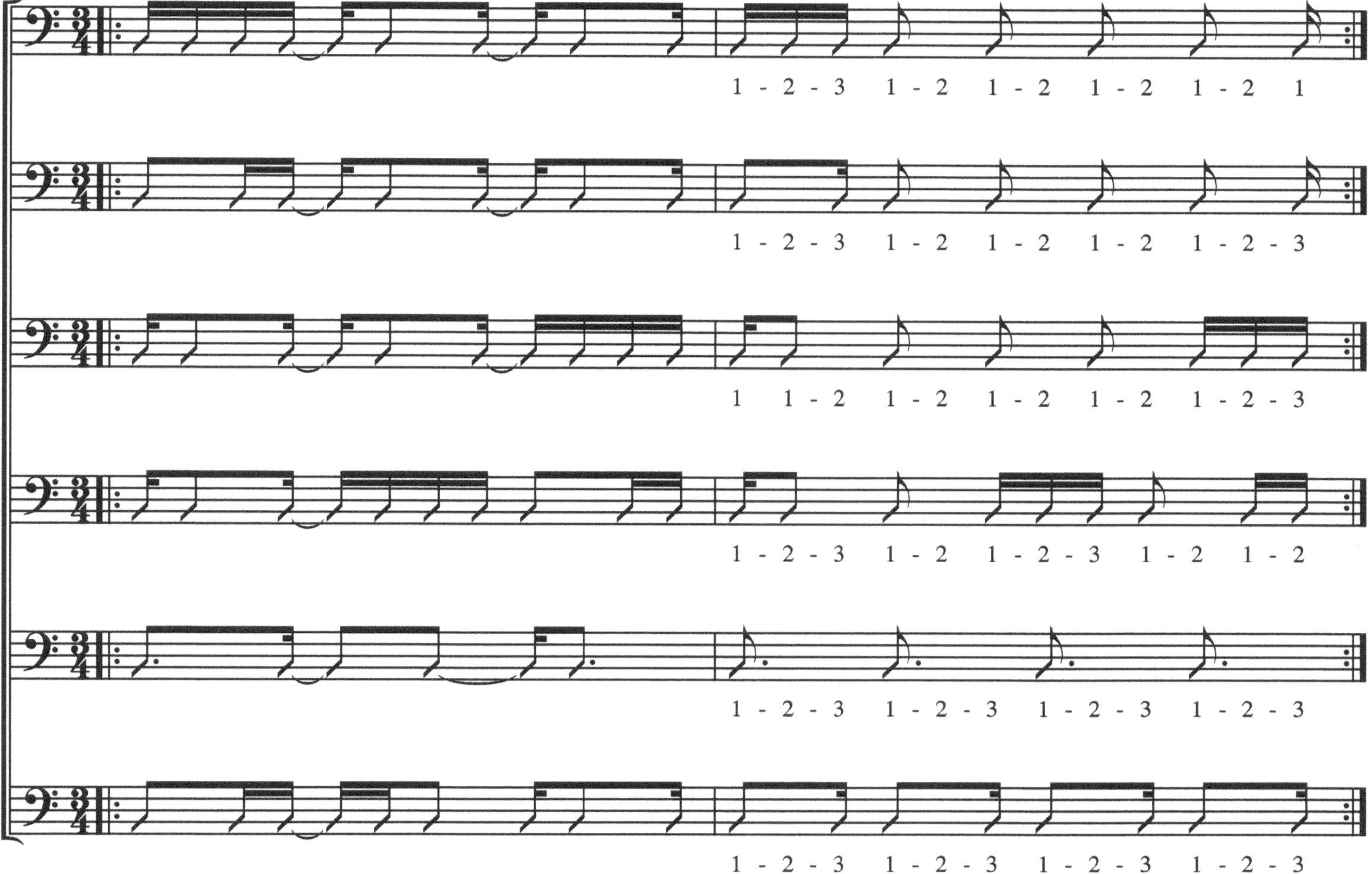

Typical ¾ Styles

The "three" feel of the waltz is very familiar. A famous ¾ composition is "On the Beautiful Blue Danube" by Johann Strauss, Jr., which is a stately waltz felt in three. At faster tempos, meters in three can be felt "in one." Sometimes up-tempo ¾ time will be felt in groups of three, such as in the jazz-waltz treatment of the Broadway show tune "My Favorite Things" as played by John Coltrane.

A slower-tempo "three" feel would be a 9/8 gospel waltz groove, with the three pulses each subdivided into three eighth notes. Rock musicians also write music based on three-beat groupings. Check out "Manic Depression" by Jimi Hendrix, which is a medium-tempo 9/8 felt in three. More recently, the tunes "The Red" by Chevelle and "So Far Away" by Staind are in a three-based meter.

Another way to group threes is into groups of two, three, or four primary pulses, each subdivided into units of three. A 6/8 meter march is felt "in two" with skipping rhythms. The University of Southern California (USC) fight song or the French national anthem, "La Marseillaise," are two common examples. The 9/8 meter is a gospel-waltz meter; 12/8 is most frequently felt as four pulses subdivided into groups of three. American gospel music and R&B ballads, as well as '50s doo-wop rock and roll, commonly employ this rhythmic feel. This type of subdividing is a way of maintaining rhythmic energy at slow tempos.

Sample $\frac{3}{4}$ Bass Lines

Let's deal with basic $\frac{3}{4}$ meter first. In example 3.4, we have a simple waltz in $\frac{3}{4}$ time felt in three. The tempo of 120 bpm is slow enough that we can feel all three quarter notes per measure. Notice that the three-quarter-note pulse is only literally expressed in the scalar walk-up in measure 8. The quarter note on beat 3 of the fourth measure rhythmically marks the middle of the eight-measure phrase. Using the pitch F in the bass line under the G chord melodically implies the dominant chord harmony. This simple bass line would be characteristic of a traditional waltz.

Example 3.4  Track 5

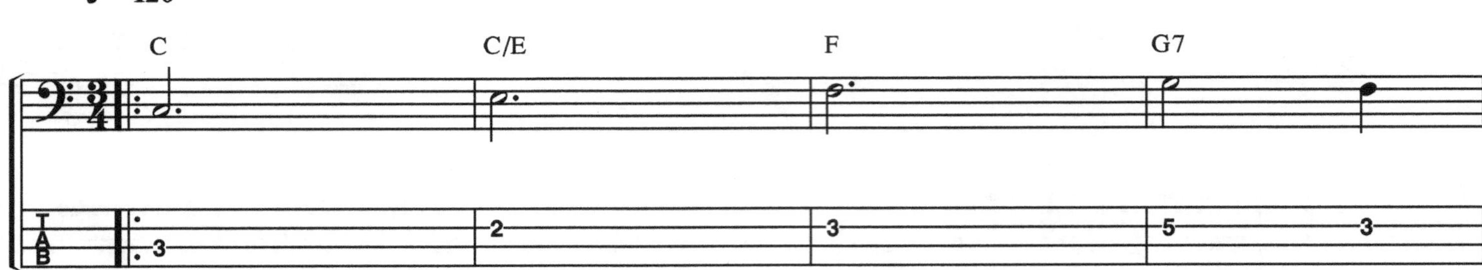

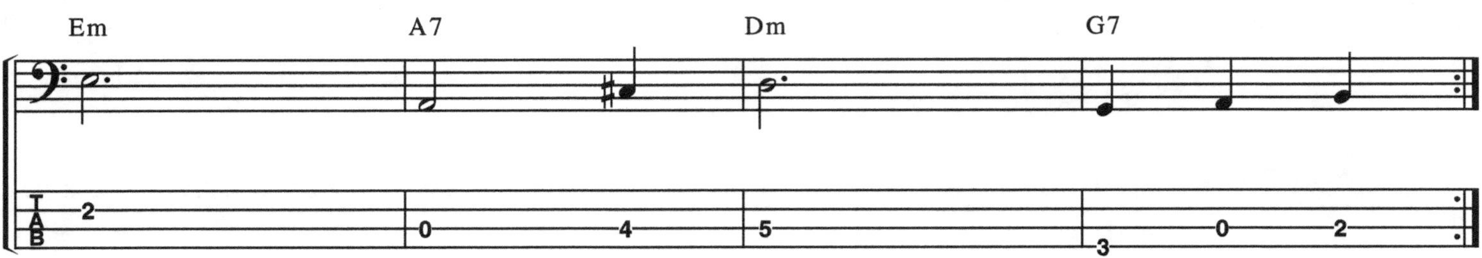

In example 3.5, we have a more harmonically complex version of example 3.4, now played as a jazz waltz. Various subdivisions of eighth notes create typical jazz syncopation. Each measure in the exercise uses a different grouping of eighths. In a real performance, you would probably want to use fewer variations at any one time and have more rhythmic repetition in a functional bass line.

Example 3.5  Track 6

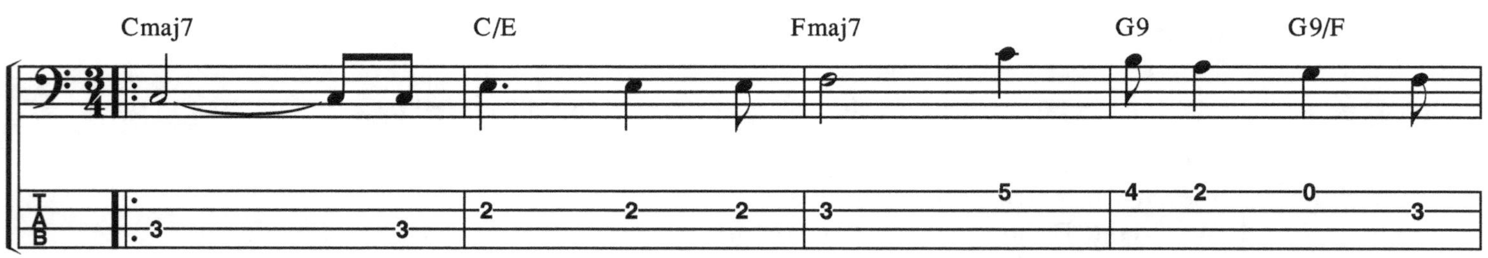

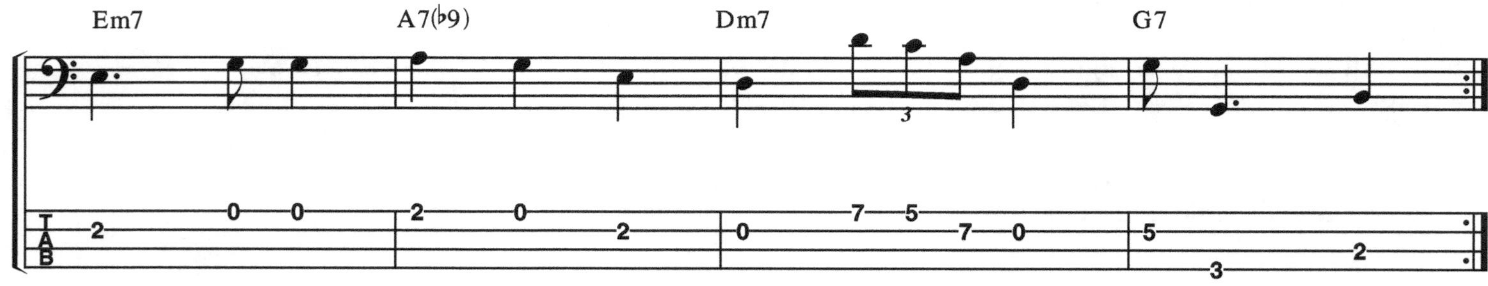

Example 3.6 is a straight eighth note rock feel. This bass line rhythmically reflects the underlying eighth-note subdivision, as is common in playing most rock styles. The moderate tempo begs for the use of more rhythmic activity in the bass line. Both this example and example 3.7 are written in $\frac{3}{4}$ meter and also contain an atypical three-measure melodic phrase.

Example 3.6 Track 7

Example 3.7 uses the same riff as example 3.6, but the bass line is constructed from a 3+3 subdivision to match the drum pattern. Measure 3 of the riff has a melodic bass fill to set up the beginning of the next three-measure phrase. Bass lines will often be composed with a larger rhythmic unit while the drums play the busy subdivisions. Because the tempo is a quick 160 bpm, we will be feeling quarter notes as the basic pulse.

Example 3.7 Track 8

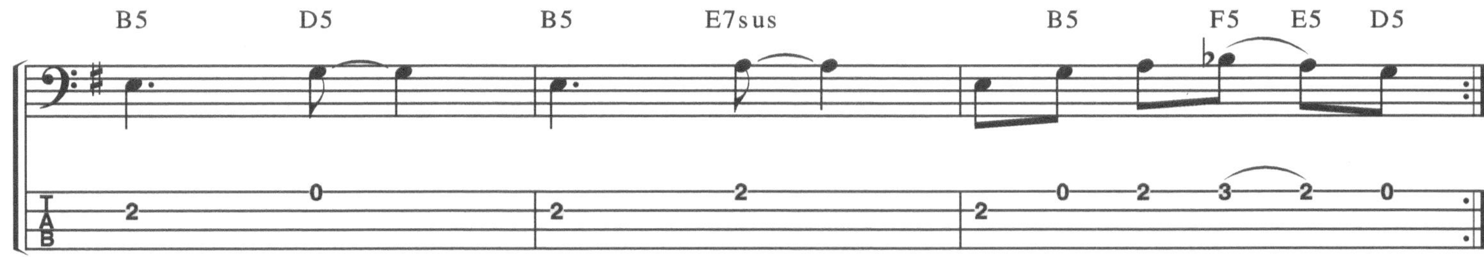

Example 3.8 uses sixteenth-note funk figures in an eight-measure phrase. The bass line is developed from a simple two-measure A–B antecedent/consequent type figure. An eight-measure phrase is created by retaining the basic idea (A) in the first measure of each two-measure phrase and varying the next figure by using four variations (B, C, D, and E) to alternate with the basic idea (A) figure. The eight-measure theme and variations bass line in example 3.8 was created with only five different one-measure licks by grouping them A-B-A-C-A-D-A-E.

Example 3.8  Track 9

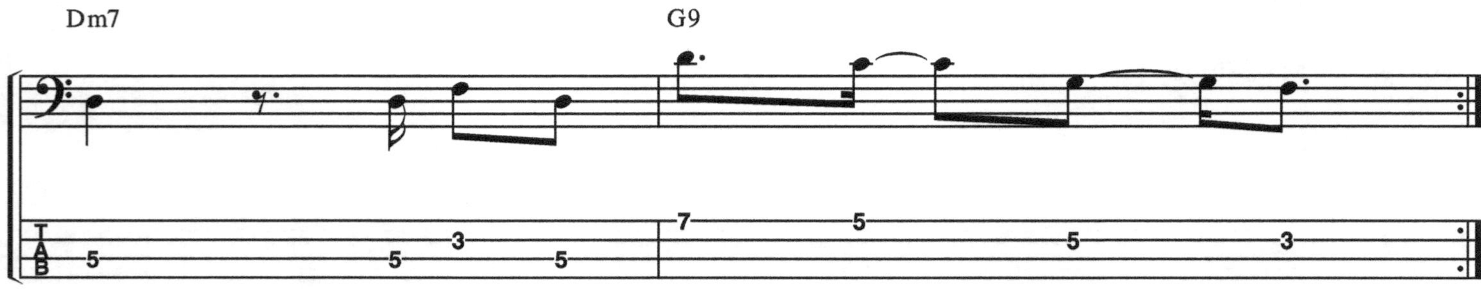

This concept of building a long, complex, and flowing bass phrase by developing a few ideas is universal in popular music. Marcus Miller, arguably the best electric funk bassist alive today, uses this compositional approach all the time. Check out "Lovin' You," the opening track from his first solo album, for a textbook demonstration of the idea, albeit in a $\frac{4}{4}$ meter.

Before we leave groups of three, we need to look at $\frac{3}{8}$ and another way to write a jazz waltz. In example 3.5, we saw a jazz waltz notated so that the quarter note indicates the basic pulse. With $\frac{3}{8}$ meter, we will have a slower basic pulse and a "one" feel with a strong accent on each group of three. Example 3.9 is played at 72 bpm (per dotted quarter). If we were to write the eighth-note pulse as quarters, it would require a frantic 216 bpm in $\frac{3}{4}$ meter. The $\frac{3}{8}$ meter imparts a lilting, buoyant rhythmic feel that is still in a three grouping. Each measure of threes gets a little accent on the downbeat.

Example 3.9 🔊 Track 10

Example 3.10 is a straight-eighth rock feel. Notice the A-B-A-C-A-D-A-E riff structure in this line and the use of "four-over-three" in the last measure of the phrase. The basic phrase is eight measures long. The last three measures are a coda created by using the "four-over-three" rhythm figure and different chords to create an ending lick.

Example 3.10 Track 11

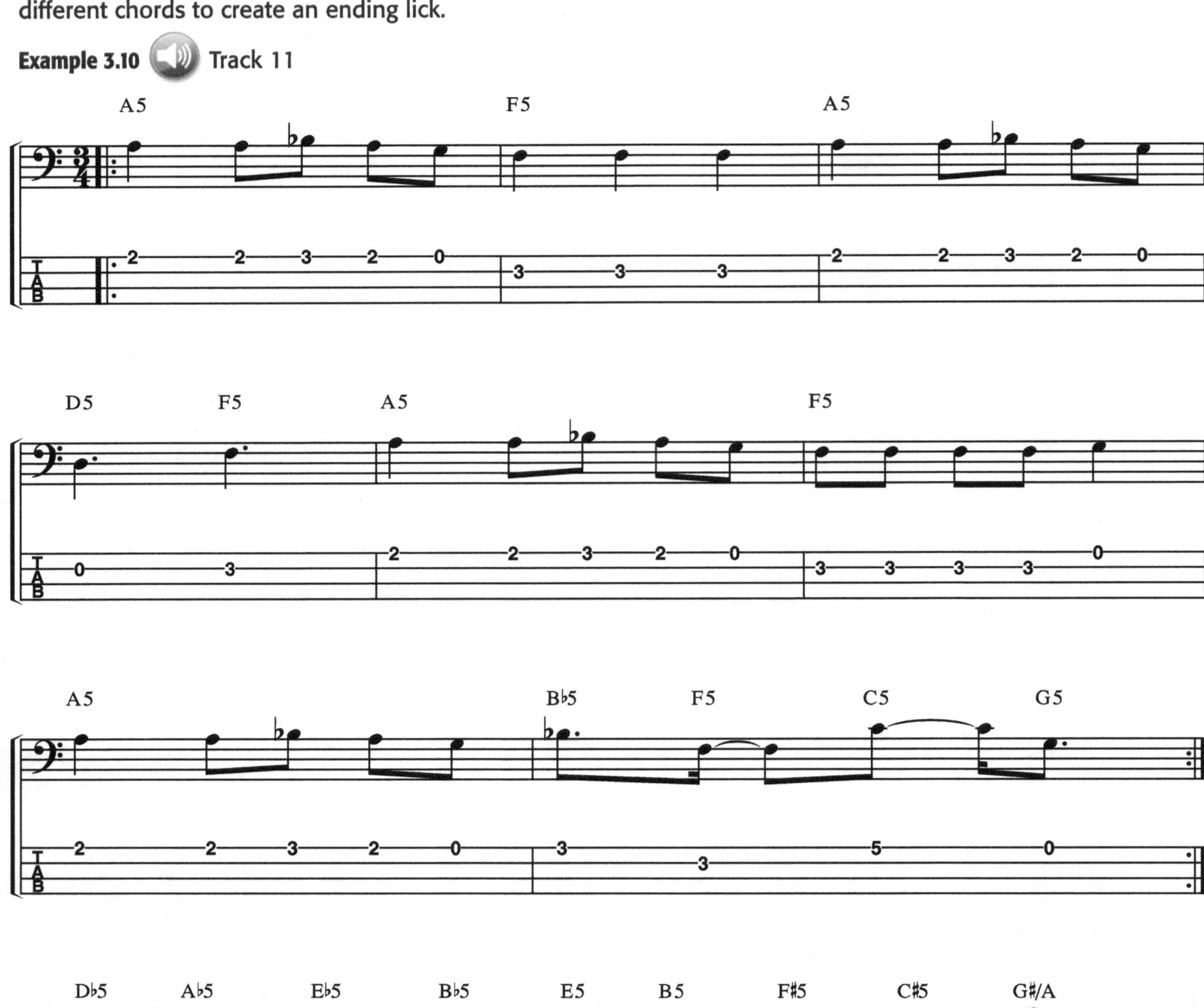

Applying the Three Steps to Mastery

It is now time to work on composing your own bass lines by applying the Three Steps to Mastery to example 3.8. Use the worksheet with the meter and the chords as a guide. The three steps will be written out this time to demonstrate the procedure as applied to example 3.8. After that, you are on your own.

1. Do the Math: Practice the basic rhythm and its subdivisions away from the bass. Use a metronome and tap or clap the rhythms. Eventually, you will be able to beat the basic meter with your feet, play the subdivisions with one hand, and play the accents at the beginning of each grouping with the other hand. Drummers do this to practice coordination. You need to use this same process to get the rhythms off the page and into your body. This physical learning stage is vitally important.

2. Learn the Chords: Learn the chord-tone arpeggios and decide which scale(s) you want to use to fill in between chord tones. Chromatic notes work well as approach tones to chord or scale notes. Example 3.11 shows the chord tones and some suggested scales.

Example 3.11

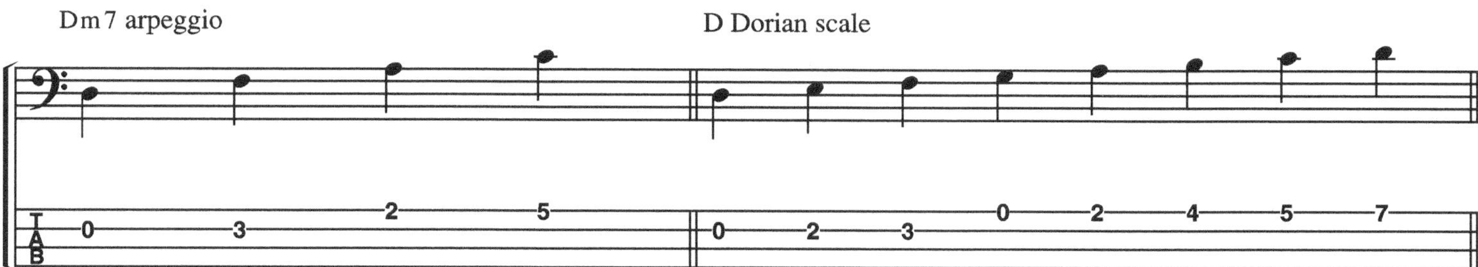

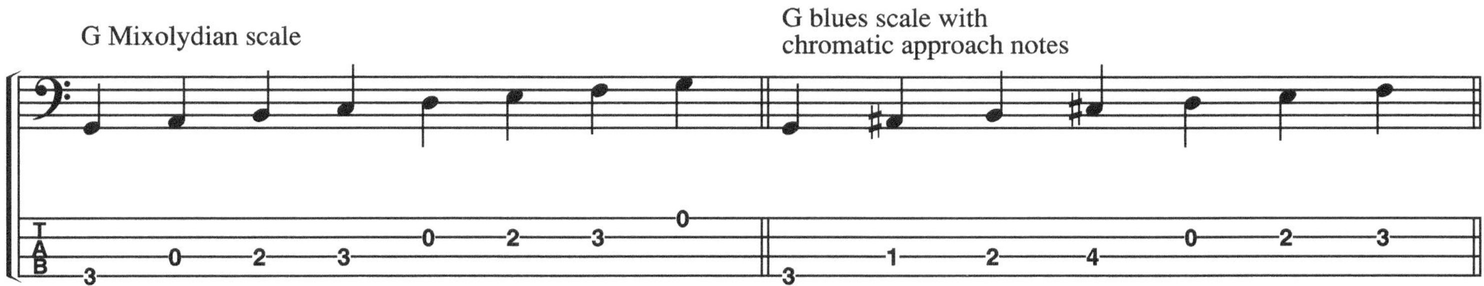

3. Put It Together: Apply your note choices to the rhythms and make music! Use the worksheet below to write out your ideas. The rhythmic style you choose will determine the kinds of bass lines you will compose. Using the theme-and-variations approach develops a melodic bass line that will also be harmonically and rhythmically supportive. From now on, you will be doing this same three-step process yourself in each meter. Repeat the track for example 3.8 and play along.

Worksheet for Example 3.8

Below is your worksheet for example 3.9. Do the Three Steps to Mastery procedure on this set of chord changes. From this point forward, you will have only the meter, chord changes, and song forms to work with. I want you to invent your own bass line rather than reproduce one I have written. Repeat the audio track for example 3.9 and create your own bass lines. Once you are confident that you know the groove, try soloing over the song form.

Worksheet for Example 3.9

Here is your worksheet for example 3.10. Use the Three Steps to Mastery procedure on this example as well. Repeat the audio track for example 3.10 and create your own bass lines. Once you're comfortable in the groove, solo over the chord changes. Try practicing by alternating between a chorus of bass lines and then a solo chorus.

Worksheet for Example 3.10

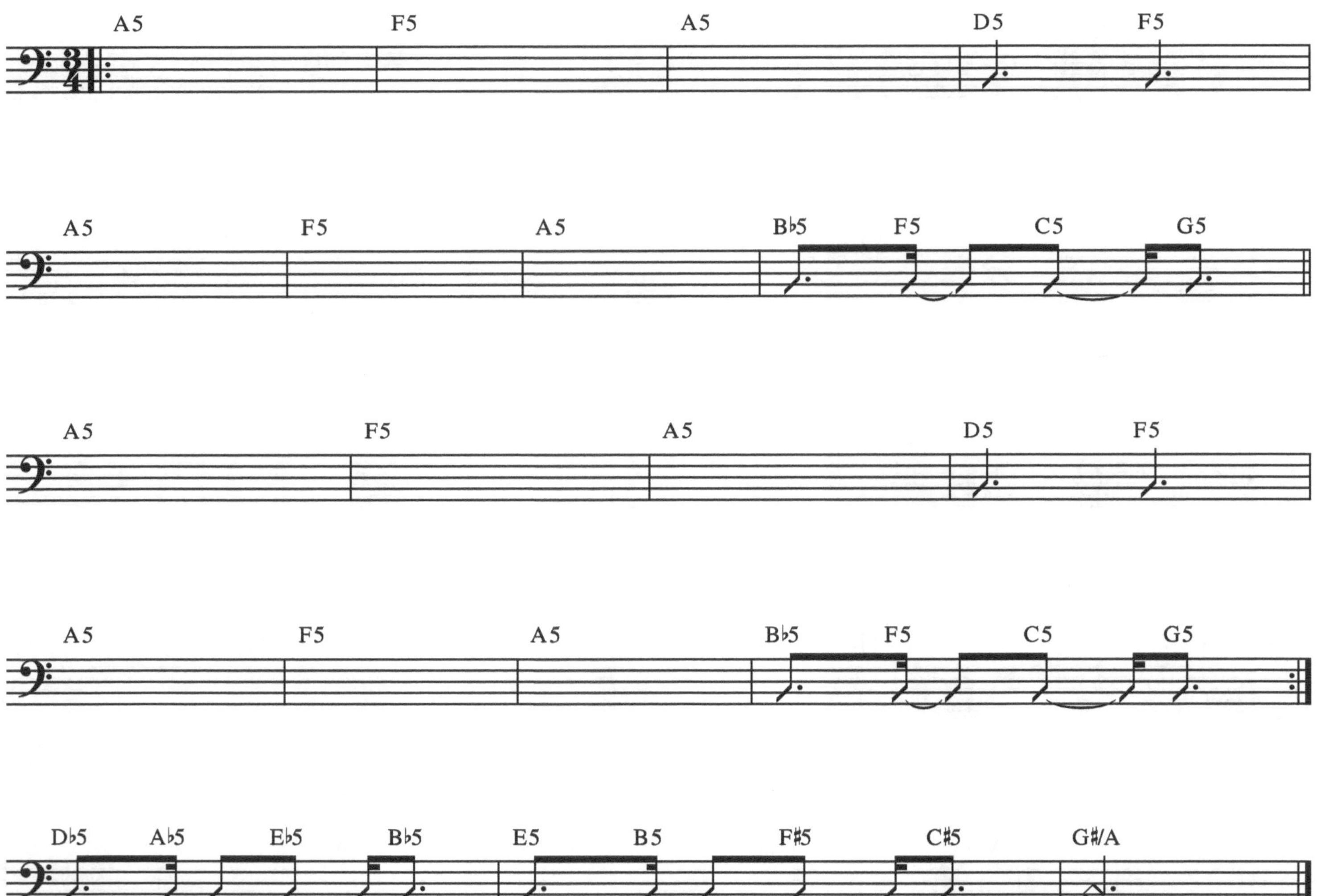

Chapter 4
Now This Is Odd: Groups of Five

Now we really will get odd by working with a five-beat rhythmic unit. We can combine one of each of our familiar groups of two and three to create a five-based meter. The common denominator rhythm could be a quarter, eighth, sixteenth, or even a half note. By far, the most common odd meter that I encounter is $\frac{5}{4}$.

Even the casual listener is probably familiar with this rhythm. Paul Desmond's jazz composition "Take Five" (performed by the Dave Brubeck Quartet in 1956) and Lalo Schiffrin's theme from the 1960s television show "Mission Impossible" are two pieces written in $\frac{5}{4}$ time. Let's start by looking at $\frac{5}{4}$ and ways to subdivide lower common denominator rhythms derived from the basic meter.

$\frac{5}{4}$ Meter

The subdivisions in example 4.1 are all based on varying groups of two and three eighth or sixteenth notes. The first line is the basic meter in quarters, then eighths. Each beginning measure of lines 2–6 contains subdivision groupings of twos or threes with accents on the downbeat of each group. The second measure of these lines shows the duration of these accented subdivision groupings written with quarter and dotted quarter notes. Lines 7–12 apply the same procedure to sixteenth-note rhythms.

Example 4.1: Rhythm Pyramid for $\frac{5}{4}$

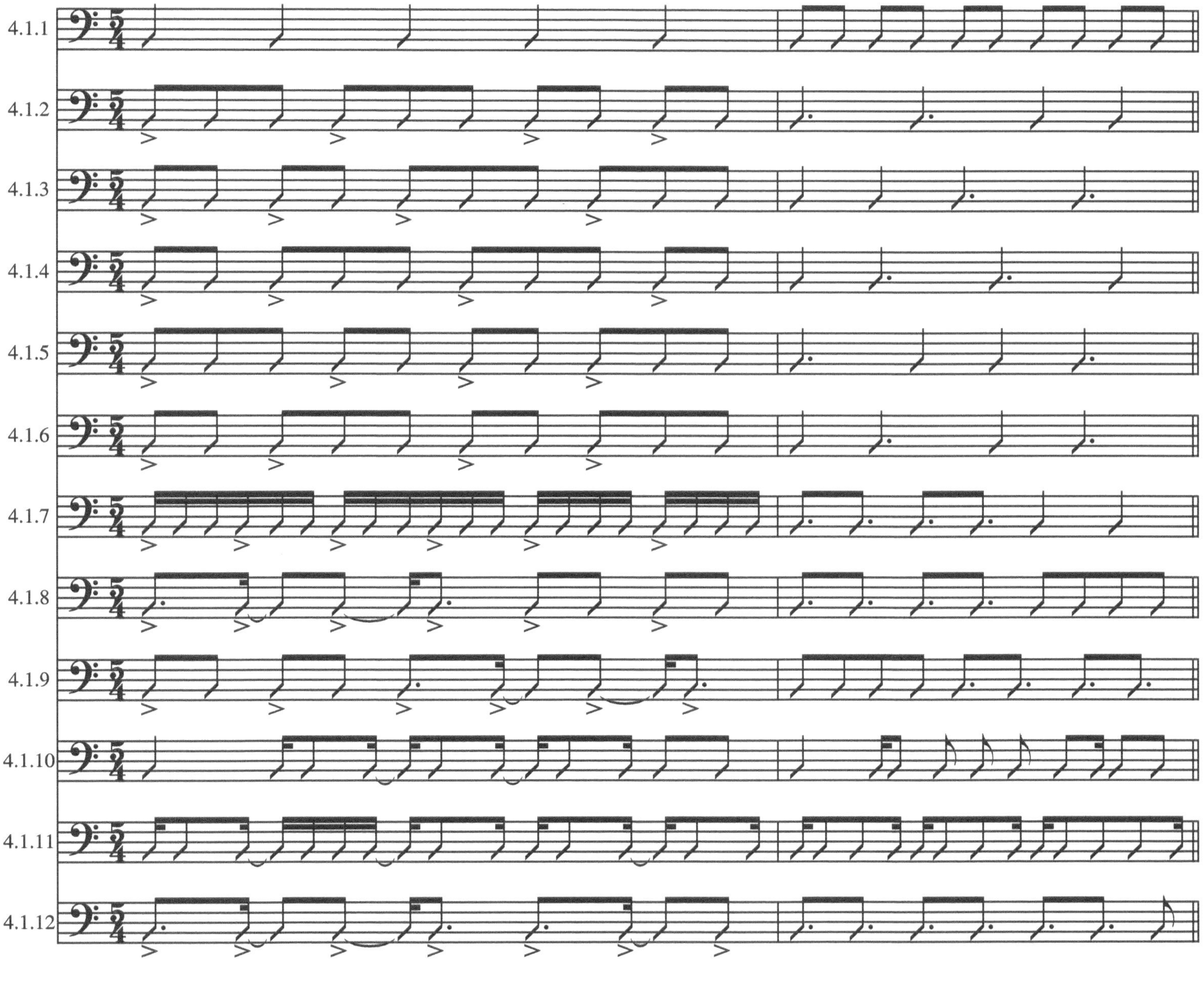

Indicating the groups of two and three is a great learning technique, so your assignment here is to take a No. 2 pencil and mark the subdivisions with 1-2 or 1-2-3 groups of either eighth notes or sixteenth notes. Thinking in subdivisions will simplify playing complex syncopated rhythms such as the one in example 4.1.11. Instead of trying to read figures written with lots of ties between the groups of four sixteenths, think in multiple groups of two or three. The result will be the actual duration of the pitches in the melodic rhythm. This melodic rhythm is what you will memorize and the one you will use to create your bass line.

Let's look at some examples of how to apply the subdivisions to chord changes. The procedure in odd meters will be to assemble phrases we have worked on in the more familiar meters of two and three from previous chapters. Once we achieve this, the hardest part is over. All the odd meters we will see later in the book will be decipherable with the material we have already covered.

Example 4.2 is based on the 3+3+2+2 subdivision. This is the "Take Five" grouping of eighth notes as shown in example 4.1.2. This is, by far, the most common grouping of $\frac{5}{4}$ that I have encountered. Notice the A-B-A-C phrase structure with a fill figure at the end of the fourth measure. Although the meter is odd, we still encounter even-numbered melodic groupings of two- or four-measure phrases. The figure in measure 8 is built around the 2+3 subdivision. Four magic dotted eighth-note rhythms are used in the 3 grouping for a unique "four-over-three" turnaround lick at the end of the eight-measure phrase.

Example 4.2  Track 12

Example 4.3 is based on the 2+2+3+3 subdivision of eighths as seen in example 4.1.3. You can hear this subdivision used in "The Grunge" by Tool. This example emphasizes the two quarter notes in the beginning of the measure. Observe the A-B-A-C melodic structure in the first four measures of the bass line. As in example 4.2, the last measure of the eight-bar phrase has a rhythmic variation from the basic pattern.

Example 4.3  Track 13

Example 4.4 is created from the 3+2+2+3 subdivision from example 4.1.5. This example is based on the rhythm used in "Methane Five" by Bryan Pezzone, composer and pianist for the band Freeflight. The first part of the example (4.4a) shows the basic groove with some variations and a melodically unique fill figure in measure 8. The second part of the example (4.4b) is created from a dotted-quarter, half, dotted-quarter (3+4+3) rhythmic figure. The resulting bass line creates a *tumbao*-like feel in $\frac{5}{4}$ without actually phrasing over the bar line as in a familiar *montuno* written in $\frac{2}{2}$ meter. ("Tumbao" refers to the typical syncopated bass line played during solos in Afro-Cuban music. "Montuno" refers to an extended vamp section for vocal and instrumental solos.)

Example 4.4a Track 14

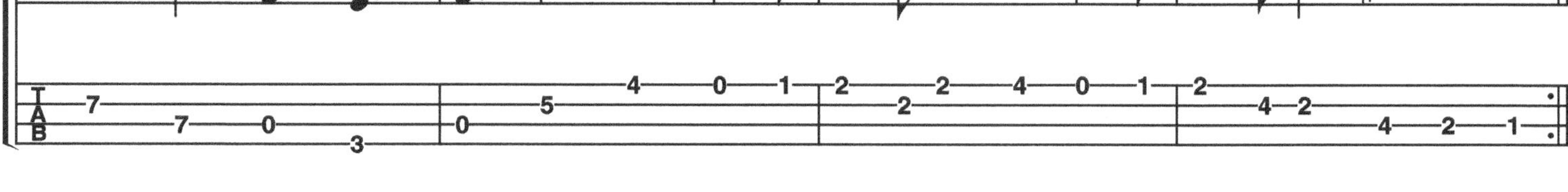

Example 4.4b

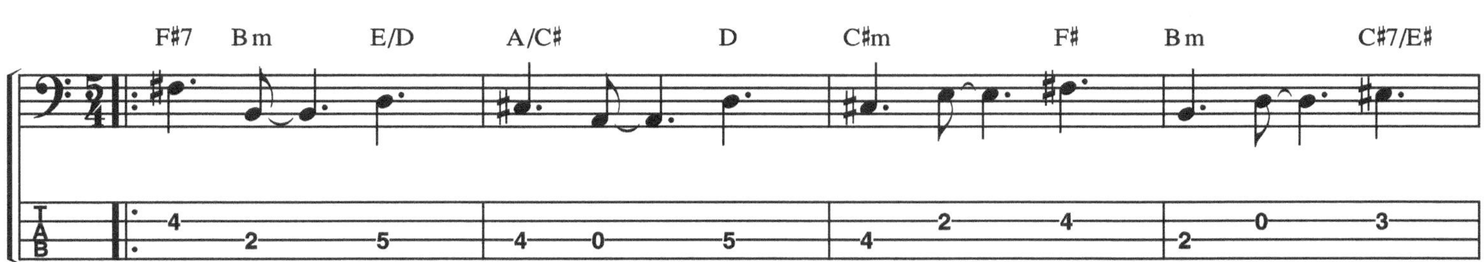

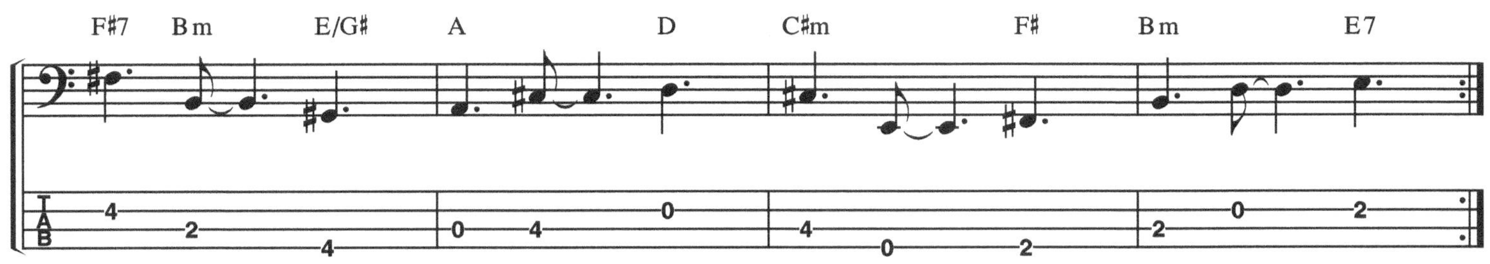

In example 4.5, we are going to create a new composition by choosing one of the subdivisions of $\frac{5}{4}$ to be the main rhythmic motive. Then we will use some of the other subdivisions as fill figures or turnaround licks.

Example 4.5  Track 15

Let's take the 3+3+2+2 subdivision and adapt a familiar **I-IV-V** blues harmony and 12-bar song form. Now use the Three Steps to Mastery and create your own bass line from the appropriate chord, scale, and chromatic tones. Finally, add melodic bass fills at the ends of four-measure phrases to set up important places in the song form, such as the **IV** chord in measure 5 or the turnaround in measure 12, and you are ready to play. Use the worksheet for example 4.5 to sketch out your own ideas.

Worksheet for Example 4.5

Please take note of several key elements in example 4.5. Notice the A-B theme and variation in the first two measures. This two-measure figure is the signature lick in the bass line. I will return to this phrase throughout the piece. Check out the tasteful use of an alternate 2+3+2+3 subdivision and a chromatic approach note leading into measure 5, an important harmonic landmark in the blues. That is when we hear the IV chord that starts the second of the three four-measure phrases that make up the 12-bar blues form.

In measures 5–8, the bass line is the signature figure we created for this tune. In bars 9–12, the last four-measure phrase, the typical V-IV-I-V cadence is played. This could call for some special bass figures to make that section melodically unique. The new lick used on the V chord (E7) is repeated on the IV chord (D7). Upon returning to the I chord in measure 7, the bass line restates the signature lick. Measure 12 features a rhythmically unique turnaround figure created from two quarters and four dotted eighths.

Before we leave this composition, take a look at example 4.6, an alternate notation version of example 4.5. There are no ties used. The note values reflect the subdivision used in each measure and what you actually hear in the melodic rhythm.

Example 4.6

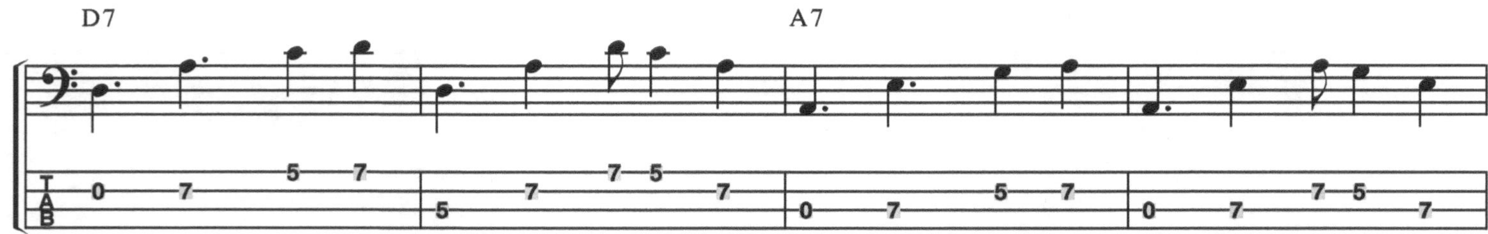

$\frac{5}{8}$ Meter

When I encounter music written in $\frac{5}{8}$ meter, it is most commonly as odd measures inserted into a mixed-meter composition alternating with another time signature such as $\frac{6}{8}$ or $\frac{2}{4}$. You will hear $\frac{5}{8}$ meter used in film or theater music for dramatic effect. An excellent example of this idea is found in the tune "Mother" by Pink Floyd. The measure of $\frac{5}{8}$ inserted into an otherwise $\frac{4}{4}$ ballad is emotionally jarring, underscoring the lyrics of obsession and despair. Music felt in five will most often be written in $\frac{5}{4}$ meter, which is easier to read and feel.

A composer might choose to write in $\frac{5}{8}$ meter to create an accent on each group of five eighths, creating more rhythmic drive. When you play in $\frac{5}{8}$, tap your foot on the quarter and the magic dotted quarter. This way you can tap your foot with two accents just as you would in $\frac{2}{4}$, except one of the groupings is an eighth note longer in duration.

Once you internalize the feel of the dotted rhythm, you will perceive the pulse in two groups— though one of the groups is longer than the other. Simple! This creates a sort of tripping or stumbling feel. This is exactly how a conductor in an orchestra makes the beat clear to the musicians when directing odd meters. Don't try to tap the odd eighth separately. It won't feel as relaxed as if you just feel two groups of alternate length.

In example 4.7, we will use a 2+3 subdivision of $\frac{5}{8}$ as the basic rhythmic motive and then use variations to highlight a desired spot in the tune. The harmony and song form are similar to "Key to the Highway," an 8-bar blues. We are using an extended version of the standard 8-bar blues form and chords. In this meter, the form becomes 24 measures. The harmonic rhythm has been stretched to fill out the $\frac{5}{8}$ meter.

Example 4.7 Track 16

Use this worksheet to sketch out rhythmic, harmonic, and melodic ideas.

Worksheet for Example 4.7

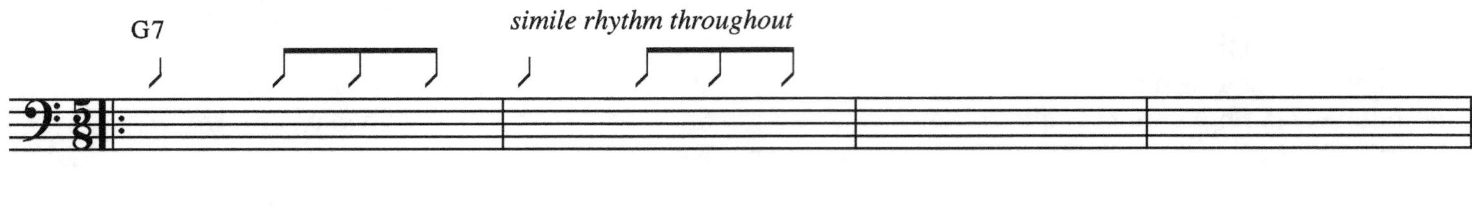

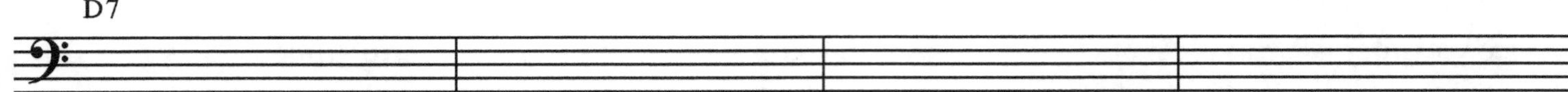

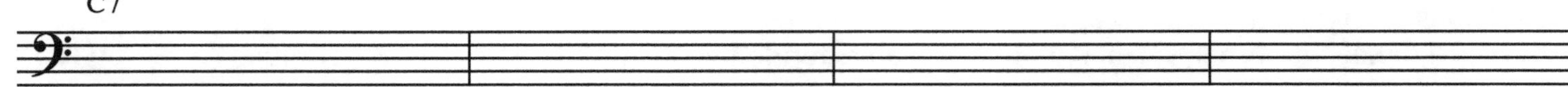

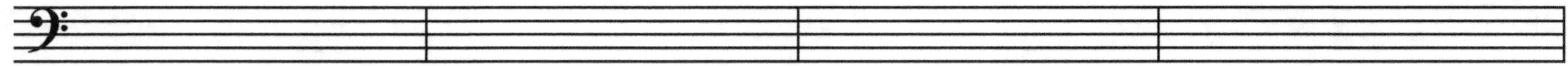

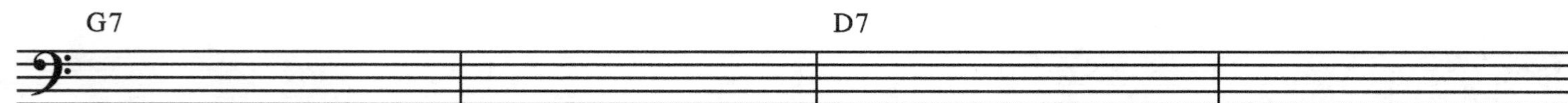

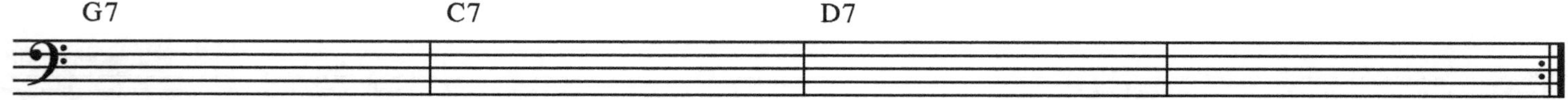

In example 4.8, we will use the opposite subdivision of 3+2. The feel is very different because the melodic rhythm of the bass line is reversed. Occasionally, I will play a separate eighth note on beat 3. Think of this note as a rhythmic approach to the last two eighths, not as a 2+3 subdivision. In this bass line, you will still want to accent the last group of two eighth notes in each measure. Notice the use of the magic dotted eighth-note rhythm in the middle of each four-measure phrase. To emphasize the turnaround, I reversed the placement of the two dotted eighth rhythms in the last four-measure phrase.

Example 4.8 Track 17

Now that we have worked on some ideas in groups of five, it is time for you to apply the concepts on your own. Remember to do the Three Steps to Mastery and start slowly. You can use the audio tracks for examples 4.5, 4.7, and 4.8 to practice. Use the worksheets provided to sketch out your ideas.

Worksheet for Example 4.8

We will meet up with $\frac{5}{4}$ and all our odd-meter friends again in chapter 9 when we work on mixed-meter compositions. Right now, let's go on to the next chapter and look at groups of seven.

Chapter 5
Seven and Seven Is: Groups of Seven

Seven is another common grouping used in odd-meter music. The longer metric unit of seven beats often feels similar to $\frac{4}{4}$ with a "skip" in the pulse. We commonly subdivide this meter into groups of 2+2+3 or 3+2+2. In my experience, the most frequently used subdivision is 2+2+3. The 2+2+3 grouping in $\frac{7}{8}$ is used in the songs "Love Is Stronger Than Justice" and "Saint Augustine in Hell" by Sting. British art-rockers Pink Floyd used a 3+2+2 subdivision of $\frac{7}{4}$ for the bass line in "Money" on their classic album *Dark Side of the Moon.* The much-less-common 2+3+2 grouping is the basis of an arrangement of Sergei Prokofiev's "Toccata" from *Piano Concerto No. 2* as performed by Freeflight.

Let's begin our exploration of seven with example 5.1. The various subdivisions are based on groups of two or three eighth notes. Rhythmic figures in the longer metric unit of seven can most often be written with easy-to-read quarter and eighth notes. If you're working in $\frac{7}{8}$, you'll commonly see more sixteenth-note rhythms. The tempo and feel of the composition will determine which meter best represents what you hear in the music.

In example 5.1, ties are used in the first measure of each example to notate the rhythmic figures. As seen in previous examples, the second measure is written without ties in the composite rhythm created by the groups of two or three. In practice, you would read the tied rhythm figures as in the first measure, but think the rhythm created by the various grouped subdivisions.

Example 5.1: Rhythm Pyramid for $\frac{7}{4}$

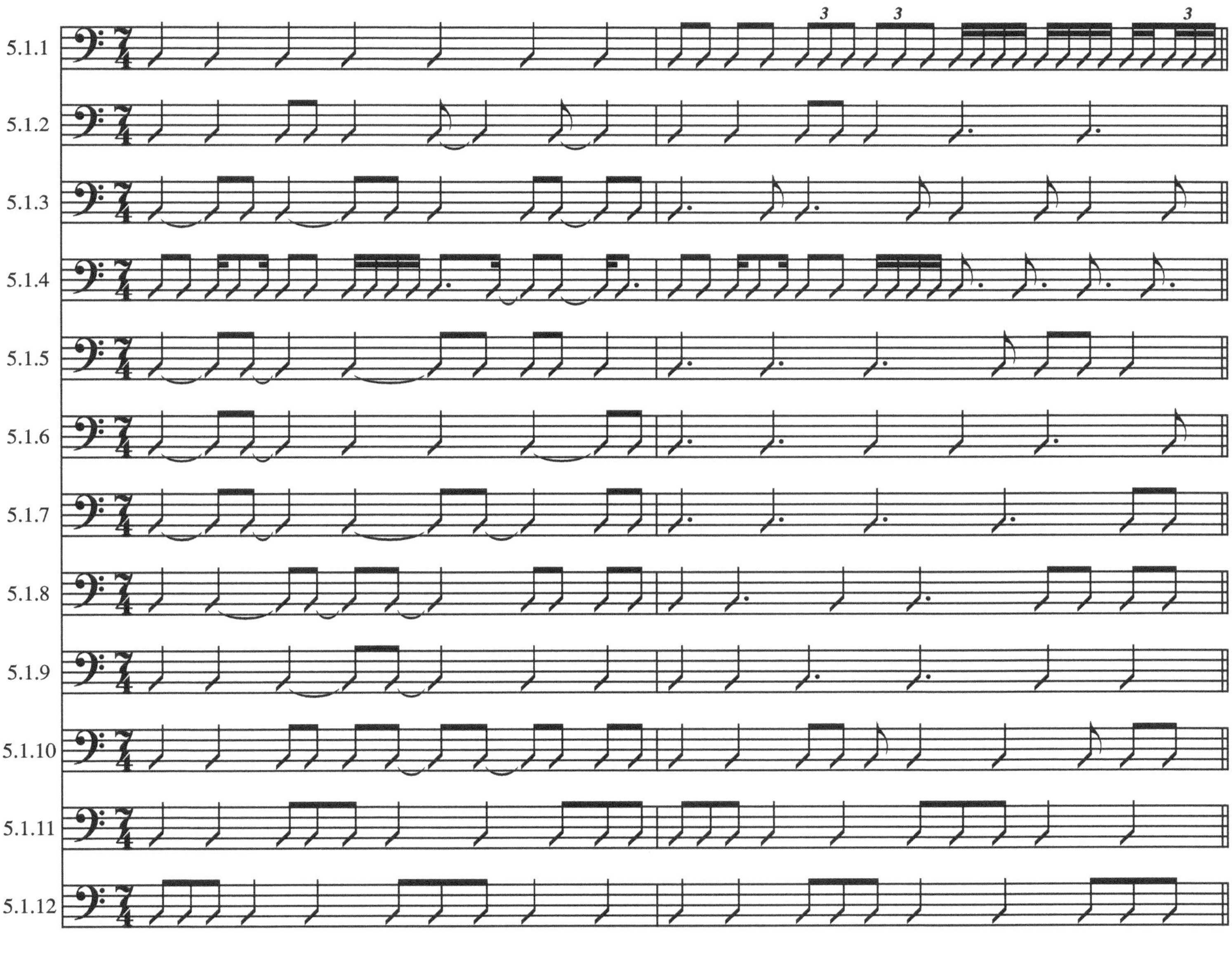

Throughout this chapter, we will refer back to the rhythm pyramid for sample motives. As stated in chapter 4, the composite melodic rhythms (the larger rhythmic groupings such as quarters and dotted quarters based on an eighth-note lowest common denominator) are the rhythms you'll use in your bass lines. Do not play every beat of the subdivisions. Leave that to the drummer to orchestrate around the drumset. This approach to rhythms facilitates creating, reading, and memorizing complex figures. I want to play a rhythmic melody, not do math problems, in a performance.

Example 5.1.1 shows the basic meter in quarter notes in the first measure, and then each quarter divided into eighths, then eighth-note triplets, sixteenths, and sixteenth-note triplets in the second measure. Example 5.1.2 introduces a phrase based on a 2+2+3 grouping of quarter notes. If I were reading the first measure, I would feel the tied notes as two dotted quarter-note rhythms as shown in the second measure. The two dotted quarters would be the rhythmic basis for lead-in fills to the next downbeat.

The rhythm in example 5.1.3 is another use of a truncated eight-beat phrase. The group of three beats at the end of the phrase provides rhythmic propulsion into the next downbeat. The theme-and-variations technique creates the A-B-A-C bass line structure that is ubiquitous in popular music. Based on the melody and the song form, pick the ideal place in the phrase for your fills. One tasteful lick in the right place is priceless. DO NOT try to compete with the drum fills and the vocal pickups. Someone will get hurt, most likely the bass player!

In example 5.2, we'll apply the rhythm of example 5.1.2 to a cliché rock guitar riff and create our bass line from the notes in the C7 chord and the C Mixolydian mode. Notice the melodic and rhythmic variation used in the lead-in figures in measures 2 and 4 of the example. Measures 5–8 of the example are written as subdivision groupings without ties, and look different but sound the same as measures 1–4.

Example 5.2 Track 18

Refer back to example 5.1.4. The same 2+2+3 subdivision of quarter notes seen in example 5.3 was assigned a set of busier sixteenth-note rhythms. This would be typical of a slower tempo than example 5.2. The slower the basic pulse, the more notes you can squeeze in. Much hip-hop music based in sixteenth-note triplets is at an *andante* tempo, 76–108 bpm.

Notice the subdivision of the last three quarter notes of the measure into four dotted eighths. Since we're working with a sixteenth note-based rhythm, we could group the last 12 sixteenths into four groups of three. This creates a driving "four-against-three" rhythmic figure to use as a lead-in to the next measure.

Example 5.3  Track 19

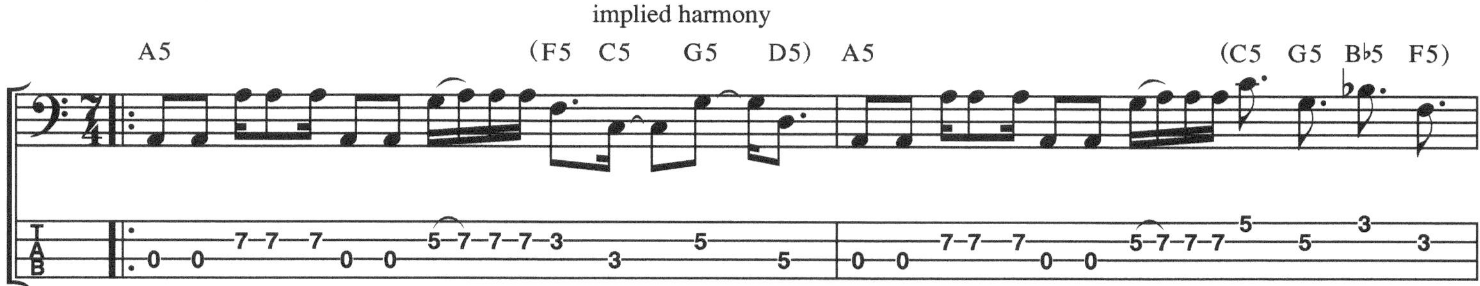

In example 5.4, we'll take the rhythm from 5.1.2 and create a primarily eighth-note rock-style bass line. The melodic structure of the bass line employs the A-B-A-C theme and variations form. Measures 1–4 are written with ties, and measures 5–8 are written without. Compare the notation for beats 5–7 of measures 2 and 6 of the example. In measure 2, the figure is written with ties between quarter notes as prescribed by the $\frac{7}{4}$ meter. Conversely, measure six is written with eighths, quarters, and dotted quarters placed anywhere within a seven-note measure.

Example 5.4  Track 20

Referring back to example 5.1, we see that 5.1.5 and 5.1.6 are based around a 3+2+2 subdivision of quarter notes. To master this rhythm, start by thinking of the eighth note as the smallest common denominator. Next, group the first six eighths of the measure into two groups of three notated as two dotted quarter notes. Playing the grouping of three at the top of the phrase produces a halting rhythmic figure that seems to hesitate and then move forward. The notation of 5.1.7 illustrates how grouping four dotted quarter notes and one lone quarter note extends this rhythmic effect.

Now, let's create a bass line from the rhythmic figures of lines 5.1.5, 5.1.6, and 5.1.7. We'll use the rhythms from all three examples to create a four-measure rhythmic motif. Use 5.1.5 as your basic rhythmic cell (A), and alternate with the rhythms of 5.1.6 (B) and 5.1.7 (C) as variations to create an A-B-A-C bass line. For pitches, we can plug in some bluesy E pentatonic riffs. Example 5.5 is our result.

Example 5.5 Track 21

We could also interpret the groups of three eighth notes in example 5.1.7 as representing music with a basic "three" feel with an odd two-beat skip at the end of the phrase; sort of a $\frac{12}{8} + 2$ groove. The dotted quarter note is now the basic unit of a predominantly "three" feel with an odd "two." For variety, we could use a contrasting subdivision rhythm for a fill figure.

In example 5.1.8 of the rhythm pyramid, we alternate between groups of two and three eighth notes. The rhythmic effect is an asymmetrical, tumbling feel that would make an ideal fill rhythm. Since it begins with a group of two eighths, it makes a good contrast to the basic "three" feel of 5.1.7, while still including two groups of three. The first two measures of example 5.6 are written with ties. The third measure is written with dotted quarters that clearly show the basic three grouping of this rhythm with the odd "two" unit at the end of the measure. I think you'll find that it is easier to think of the bass line in the reduced subdivision groupings.

Example 5.6 Track 22

Here's the compositional process used to create example 5.6. First, we use the rhythm of example 5.1.7 as our basic motive. Then, we use the rhythmic figure in 5.1.8 for a fill in the last measure of a four-measure phrase. This way we create an A-A-A-B bass line that has rhythmic repetition balanced with variation. The last two eighth notes of measures 1, 2, and 3 are the odd "two" grouping in a primarily "three" feel. We can take advantage of this repeated eighth-note rhythm to create melodic variety. The two eighths are played differently in each measure, with melodic variations created from the E minor pentatonic scale.

In example 5.7, we'll employ a $\frac{5}{4}$ plus $\frac{2}{4}$ phrase and use a common song form, the 12-bar minor blues, to produce a new take on some very familiar material. The rhythmic figure shown in example 5.1.9 is based on the 2+3+2 subdivision of seven quarter notes. By sounding the "three" groups of notes as two dotted quarters, we will have six articulations within a seven-beat measure. The eighth notes then are grouped 2+2+3+3+2+2. This juxtaposition of two dotted-quarter notes between two groups of two quarters produces a symmetric bookend-type rhythmic figure. Hearing the two dotted quarter notes followed by two quarters also suggests the common 3+3+2+2 eighth-note subdivision of $\frac{5}{4}$ as seen in example 4.2.

Example 5.7 Track 23

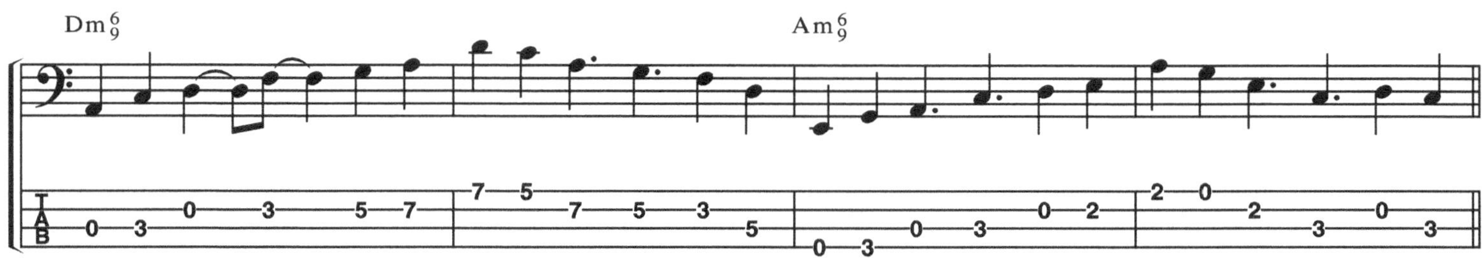

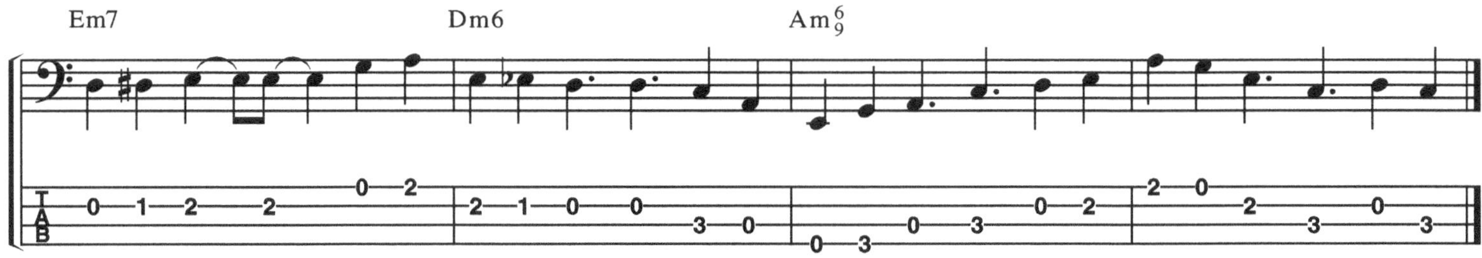

In example 5.8, we have a phrase built from seven quarter notes grouped 4+3. This bass line is a variation of an ostinato blues bass riff. The group of three quarters is played with an eighth-note subdivision of 2+1+2+1 that creates a syncopated fill figure at the end of each measure. The basic impression is that of a two-measure phrase in $\frac{4}{4}$ with a note missing at the end of the phrase. The last measure of the eight-measure phrase is a contrasting rhythm based on 3+2+2+2+2+3 eighth notes. The notation of measure 8 clearly shows the groups of three eighth notes surrounding a familiar four-quarter-note arpeggiated riff.

Example 5.8 Track 24

Example 5.9 is another example of seven quarter notes grouped 4+3; however, in this example, the tempo is slower than example 5.8 and the rhythmic feel is sixteenth-note funk. Each measure of this bass line has a slight variation on the basic riff in measure 1.

Example 5.9 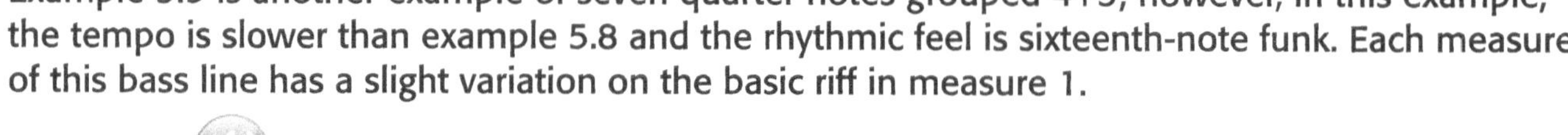 Track 25

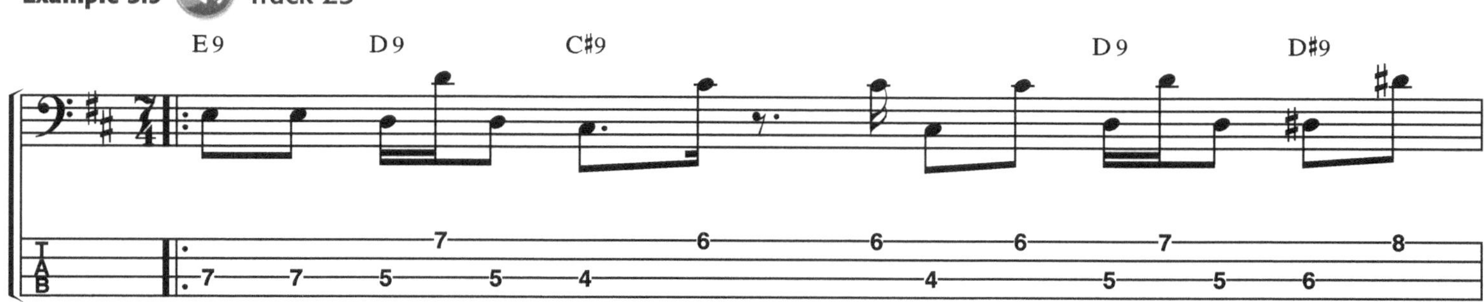

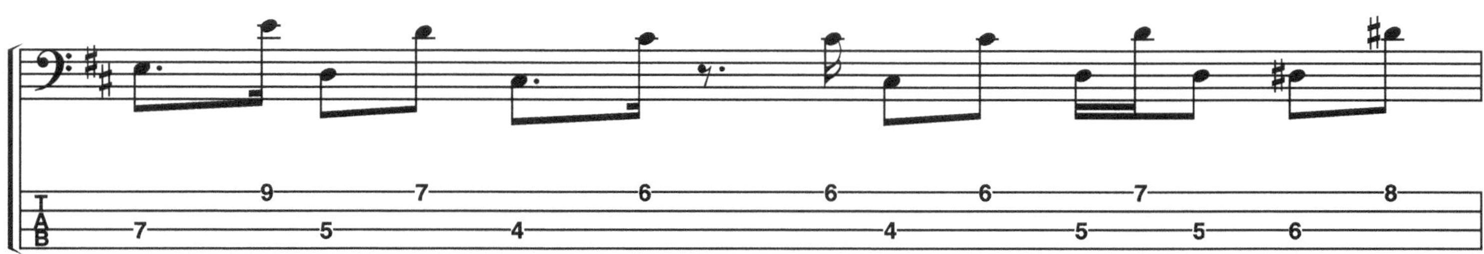

The last example, example 5.10, is based on a 2+2+3+2+2+3 grouping of eighth notes as seen in example 5.1.10. As mentioned earlier in this chapter, any of our $\frac{7}{4}$ rhythms could be notated, alternatively, in $\frac{7}{8}$. Notating this particular bass line in $\frac{7}{4}$ means that we see half as many bar lines as in $\frac{7}{8}$. Using $\frac{7}{4}$ meter also means that each measure will represent a complete musical phrase. If you were to write out this bass line, you would be free to choose which meter best represents the music you hear.

The first four measures of example 5.10 are in $\frac{7}{4}$, and then we switch to $\frac{7}{8}$ notation in measures 5–12 for purposes of comparison. As seen in examples 5.1.11 and 5.1.12, you could vary the order of two- and three-beat groups and create many interesting variations for fills and different sections of the composition. Check out the last two measures of the $\frac{7}{8}$ section to see this concept applied to this example.

Example 5.10 Track 26

Now that you have worked on some seven-beat rhythmic units, it's time for you to apply these concepts yourself. Write a worksheet and play the examples using the audio tracks to practice your playing and improvising skills. **Start slowly.** (I know I said I wasn't going to mention it again, but… use a metronome.) Use the Three Steps to Mastery and all will be well. Once you're full of seven, go to the next chapter to examine rhythms in groups of nine.

Chapter 6

Number Nine: Groups of Nine

We skipped meters in six ($\frac{6}{8}$ and $\frac{6}{4}$) because we covered triple meters in chapter 3. In fact, meters in six are not odd-meter at all. Usually, $\frac{6}{8}$ represents a "two" feel with an underlying triplet subdivision. Marches are sometimes written in $\frac{6}{8}$ meter. Rock songs such as "Whip It" by Devo would be notated in $\frac{6}{4}$ time; basically an extended $\frac{4}{4}$ phrase. The time we spent in compound or triple meter will help us now understand nine-based meters.

Nine-beat groupings are really fun to play. There are many possible groupings of twos and threes with which to create interesting syncopations. Music based on nine-beat groupings can be felt as an elongated $\frac{4}{4}$ rhythmic phrase. You *could* feel the music as duple time with an extended rhythmic grouping (2+2+2+3). You could also feel the time as a triple meter with a triplet subdivision (3+3+3). You can create interesting asymmetrical phrases by mixing even and odd subdivisions (2+3+2+2 or 3+2+2+2).

Metric notation is supposed to represent the basic pulse of a musical composition. The faster the tempo, the larger the notation unit used to represent what we hear and feel. Marches, Broadway show tunes, sambas, and Afro-Caribbean or salsa music are commonly written in cut time ($\frac{2}{2}$) if the tempo is fast. Complex syncopations can be written with easier-to-read quarters and eighth notes. Funk music, which typically has a slower basic pulse, is usually written in $\frac{4}{4}$ meter, and the busy rhythms are represented with eighth and sixteenth notes.

Meters can be written with any rhythmic value as the lower denominator, from a whole note (e.g., $\frac{2}{1}$) to a thirty-second note (e.g., $\frac{9}{32}$). I have seen these meters in modern symphonic pieces and film scores, but this is not a common practice in commercial music. In the real world, you will most frequently see nine-beat meters notated in $\frac{9}{8}$.

A nine-beat unit is beginning to be too much to look at if the quarter note is the basic rhythmic denominator. Measures with seven- and nine-beat phrases are sometimes written with a dotted bar line somewhere within the measure to show the subdivision of the phrase, or, as in "A Soldier's Tale" by Igor Stravinsky, subdivisions are beamed over the bar line.

We'll begin our journey to Nine with example 6.1, various rhythms in $\frac{9}{4}$. The larger quarter- and eighth-note rhythms are easier to read than sixteenths in $\frac{9}{8}$. Ties will be used in each first measure, and the subdivision groupings of two or three will be individually notated in the second measure of each line. We won't do as complete a rhythmic breakdown in nine. The work you did with groups of two and three is simply compounded now in a larger grouping. The rhythms are more complex now, so subdivision groupings will begin with the second example, just as in the $\frac{5}{4}$ and $\frac{7}{4}$ rhythm pyramids.

Example 6.1: Rhythm Pyramid for $\frac{9}{4}$

Example 6.1.1 shows the basic rhythm in quarter notes, and then shows them written as eighths, triplets, sixteenths, and sixteenth-note triplets in the second measure. Example 6.1.2 is based on a 2+2+2+3 grouping of nine. The dotted quarters in the second measure will provide rhythmic momentum into the next phrase. Examples 6.1.3 (2+2+3+2) and 6.1.4 (2+3+2+2) are also duple feels with the odd three group moved around in the measure.

Applying the magic dotted rhythm concept to any three group and playing "two-over-three" will produce a propulsive syncopated figure. Thinking the dotted-rhythm figure is an easy way to handle the "odd" piece of the overall phrase. Drummers keep time by rocking their foot toe to heel. In $\frac{9}{4}$, I would tap out the primary groups of two and the two dotted rhythms created from the three group. When you tap with your foot, the time feel is expressed in your body, and you're freed from counting in your head.

Example 6.1.5 of the pyramid is a 3+3+3 grouping. If you are playing a nine-beat melodic or harmonic phrase with an eighth-note rock feel, you would want to use the $\frac{9}{4}$ notation. You'll commonly see this 3+3+3 grouping written in $\frac{9}{8}$ as the standard notation for a gospel waltz, which is a "three" feel with an underlying triplet rhythm.

For our first bass line example, let's use the rhythm of 6.1.2 as the basis for example 6.2, a samba in $\frac{9}{4}$. The basic feel is in two, with an extra skip in the pulse. Notice the various uses of typical dotted-quarter plus eighth-note figures on the groups of two and the combinations of eighths and quarters in the three grouping.

Example 6.2  Track 27

Moderate samba

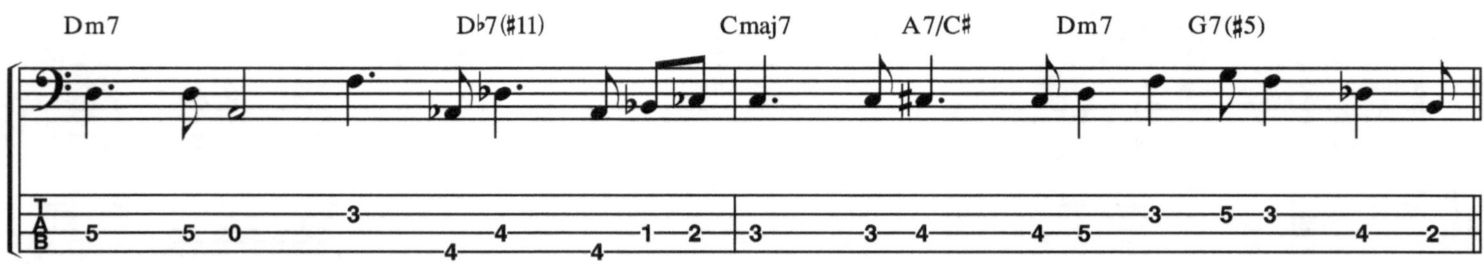

Example 6.3 is based on the 3+3+3 grouping. The feel is eighth-note rock, so the notation is in $\frac{9}{4}$. You could write this in $\frac{3}{4}$ meter, but the harmonic phrase is actually nine beats. The $\frac{9}{4}$ meter reflects the rhythmic feel, the slow tempo, and the real musical phrase with 66.666% fewer bar lines. The first measure uses ties to join eighth notes within the notation of nine even quarter notes. The second measure is written to reflect the subdivisions of the nine beats into three groups of three. Notice the A-B-A-C-A-B-A-D melodic structure of the eight-measure bass line.

Example 6.3 Track 28

Moderate rock

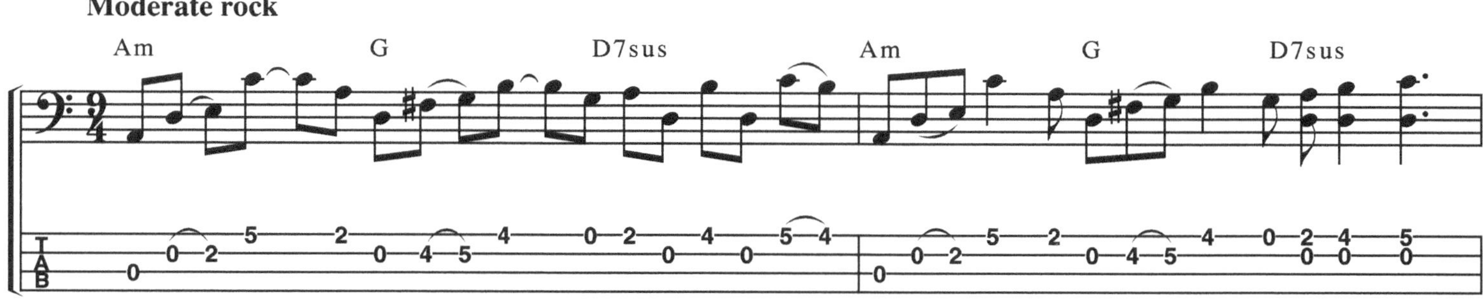

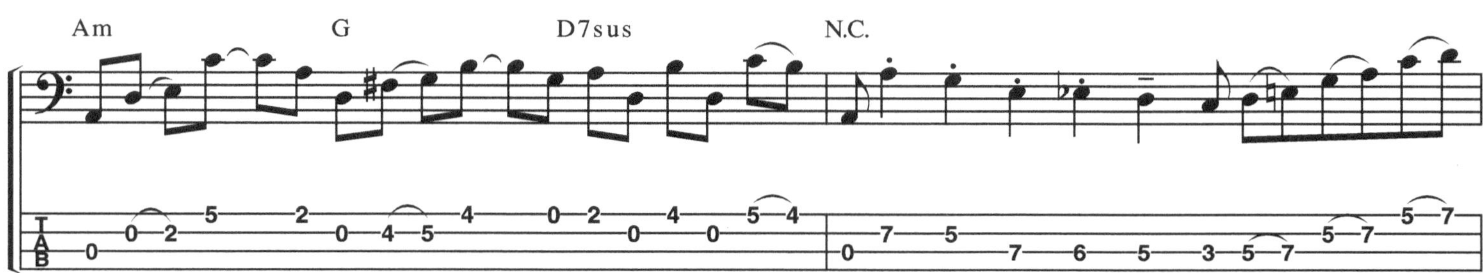

In example 6.4, the 2+2+3+2 grouping is used. The melodic phrase begins with a 4+3+2 organization of melodic cells. The bracketed numbers over the bar in this example show the variations of the basic grouping of 4+3+2. The eighth measure contains an ensemble lick that acts as a turnaround to the beginning of the phrase. The eighth-note notation is characteristic of this type of rock music. Using an odd meter can produce a fresh take on familiar riffs and chord changes. We'll use a G9 chord form and create the bass line from blues licks based on the G Mixolydian mode.

Example 6.4  Track 29

Example 6.5 shows how some of the groupings from example 6.1 look in $\frac{9}{8}$. We'll now start working with sixteenth notes to subdivide a basic eighth-note pulse. Example 6.5.1 is the 2+2+2+3 subdivision used extensively in "Blue Rondo a la Turk" written by Dave Brubeck. This song and "Take Five" by Paul Desmond popularized odd meters in the jazz idiom. Check out the breakthrough album *Time Out* by the Dave Brubeck Quartet, originally released in 1956. "Blue Rondo a la Turk" alternates the use of the 2+2+2+3 subdivision with figures grouped in 3+3+3 and, finally, straight $\frac{4}{4}$ swing for rhythmic variety.

Example 6.5

Example 6.5.2 is based on the 2+2+2+3 grouping and would be another way to write a samba in nine as seen in example 6.2. In the first measure, the three-group rhythm is written with ties, and in the second measure, with dotted eighths. Examples 6.5.3 and 6.5.4 involve moving the odd group of three beats within a basic "two" feel. You have four possibilities. Any one measure could be the basis for a groove figure with any other measure used as a basis for a contrasting fill figure. Dozens of great combinations are possible using the theme-and-variations concept. Example 6.5.5 is a rhythm you'd hear in gospel waltzes that have a triplet interpretation of a basic "three" pulse.

Example 6.6 uses the 2+2+2+3 subdivision of 6.5.2 as the basic groove figure for three measures, and the 3+3+3 grouping as a fill figure in the last measure of a four-measure phrase. Notice the A-B-A-C melodic theme and variations construction of the bass line. Listen for how the 3+3+3 grouping propels the figure into the top of the next phrase. The melodic material is derived from an A blues scale.

Example 6.6 Track 30

Example 6.7 is based on the 3+2+2+2 grouping of eighth notes seen in the second measure of 6.5.4. The rhythmic effect is one of $\frac{3}{8} + \frac{3}{4}$ in each measure. As we saw in example 6.6, the melodic riff is based on the A blues scale. Placing the group of three at the beginning of the measure produces the rhythmic equivalent of stumbling at the top of the phrase. Contrast this effect with the leading quality created by playing the group of three at the end of the measure, as seen in measures 7 and 8 of this example.

Example 6.7 Track 31

Example 6.8 is based on the 3+3+3 subdivision of $\frac{9}{8}$, as seen in example 6.5.5. This is a common feel in gospel music and R&B ballads. We feel the pulse as three groups of three. If you have a 3+3+3 grouping as your groove unit, any one of the other subdivision measures could be used to create a strong fill figure into the next phrase. These essential concepts of theme and variations and setting up the next phrase are fundamental. Listen to your favorite bass players, in any style of music, and you'll hear them using these compositional devices to create great bass lines.

Example 6.8 Track 32

Moderato

Example 6.9 is created from a 2+2+3+2 grouping of eighth notes as seen in the second measure of 6.5.3. The harmony is a common rock chord progression. Notice the A-B-A-C melodic phrasing of the bass line.

Example 6.9 Track 33

Example 6.10 shows four options you have to place the group of three anywhere within a predominantly "two" feel. This technique creates surprising rearrangements of the accented notes. In this example, the group of three is always played as two dotted eighths, so it is easy to see where they fall within the measure. The rhythmic placement of the group of three within the measure sometimes creates forward momentum, and sometimes creates a stumbling, halting effect. To aid in understanding the moving rhythmic accents in the bass line, I've used the most common, clichéd disco riff as my melodic material.

Example 6.10 Track 34

Now that we've worked on nine-beat rhythmic units, it's time for you to apply these concepts yourself. Create your own worksheets and practice with the audio tracks. Repeat a track and play alternate phrases of a bass line and then a solo, over and over. This will hone your playing and improvising skills. Writing ideas out with a pencil frees up processing power in your brain. Use the Three Steps to Mastery and start out of tempo, if necessary. Increase the tempo slowly as you become more proficient.

If you write music, try this technique: Play an odd-numbered melodic phrase, such as one in $\frac{9}{8}$, with the melodic instruments over a simple duple meter, like $\frac{2}{4}$, in the drums. This technique will create a melodic phrase that will begin on a downbeat in the first measure of a two-measure phrase and an upbeat in the second measure. Finally, the lick starts again on a downbeat in the next two-measure phrase. The effect is that the melodic riff "turns around," or goes in and out of phase relative to the basic groove and then turns back around, creating a nifty syncopated figure. If the drum beat is a simple $\frac{2}{4}$ pattern, the figure will complete a phase cycle within two beats. Check out "Black Dog" by Led Zeppelin to hear this idea at work.

Try taking a familiar $\frac{4}{4}$ figure and adding one beat's worth of notes. Begin by adding the extra beat at the end of the phrase to produce a group of three at the end of a common lick. Apply the magic dotted rhythm concept to the group of three. Then move the odd bit to a different place in what would otherwise be a simple $\frac{4}{4}$ phrase. Tap your foot on the primary beats of the subdivision and the dotted rhythms. Use a drum machine or metronome to practice. Go ahead and have fun—lose track of time (on the clock that is).

Once you're comfortable in nine-beat meters, go on to the next chapter to examine rhythms in groups of eleven.

Chapter 7
Die Elf: Groups of Eleven

I love this meter! Songs in eleven are reminiscent of those in seven. Just as seven-beat phrases can feel like $\frac{4}{4}$ minus a beat, $\frac{11}{8}$ suggests a $\frac{12}{8}$ meter with one beat dropped. This similarity to a common meter can be an advantage when we want to revisit familiar harmonic and melodic material with a fresh rhythmic feel. We have literally dozens of interesting rhythmic options in eleven-based meters.

Meters with a large odd denominator of beats (such as $\frac{11}{8}$) are referred to as *asymmetric additive metric patterns* by musicologists. Béla Bartók, a famous 20th-century composer, used Balkan folk music as a basis for pieces in his *Mikrokosmos* piano suite. He notated the asymmetric additive meters in his compositions in groups such as $\frac{2+2+3}{8}$ and $\frac{3+2}{8}$ rather than $\frac{7}{8}$ or $\frac{5}{8}$.

As we observed in chapter 6 when we looked at groups of nine, we can group twos and threes to imply a basically duple (2) or triple (3) meter with an odd bit somewhere in the phrase. In this chapter, we'll have eleven beats to play with, and that affords us many more rhythmic possibilities. For the last chapters of the book, we'll dispense with writing these basic rhythms with ties. By now, you are familiar with how to use the subdivision concept to interpret tied rhythms.

Example 7.1: Rhythm Pyramid for $\frac{11}{8}$

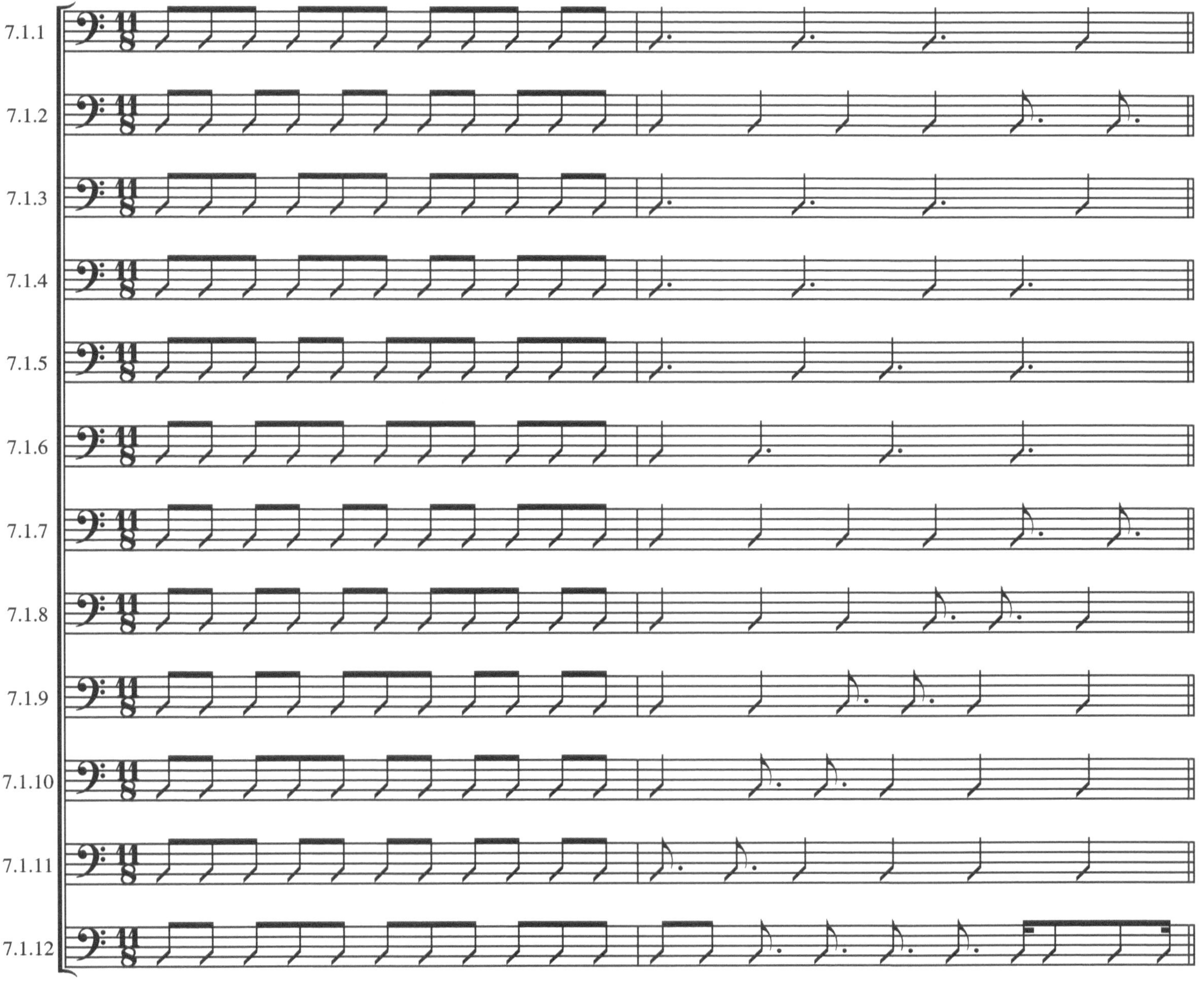

Starting with these groups of eleven, we'll start thinking with eighth-note subdivisions. We're not going to use $\frac{11}{4}$ notation in this chapter. The rhythmic phrase has become so long in $\frac{11}{4}$ that, unless the tempo is very fast, I find it easier to think of any eleven-based groupings with the $\frac{11}{8}$ meter.

Example 7.1.1 shows how eleven can be grouped as 3+3+3+2. The eighths are displayed in groups in the first bar and then in composite subdivision notation in the second. Grouped this way, we have an odd-time measure that contains an even number of articulations. The three dotted quarters are equal in length, and the quarter has the short duration—the odd bit. If I were playing in this meter, I would tap my foot toe to heel on these four primary groupings instead of trying to count to eleven. It's *so* much easier.

Example 7.1.2 shows a 2+2+2+2+3 subdivision in the first measure and the composite rhythm in the second measure. Since I had a group of three within a primarily "two" meter, I used the magic dotted rhythm spell on the three eighths and turned my odd ugly duckling grouping into two beautiful even dotted eighths. Now this example contains six articulations, four equal and two slightly shorter units of time.

Examples 7.1.3 through 7.1.6 show the predominantly triplet-type feel with a "two" group moved earlier in each measure. There are four rhythmic possibilities for any measure. You could get sixteen different four-measure combinations by mixing and matching rhythms.

Examples 7.1.7 through 7.1.11 conversely show a predominantly duple rhythmic milieu with a group of three moved to a different place in each measure. The three-note grouping will be subdivided into two dotted rhythms for these exercises to maintain an even number of articulations per measure. Example 7.1.12 combines groups of twos and threes, and introduces a syncopated sixteenth-note figure on the group of three.

As I mentioned earlier, the most practical application of eleven will be as either a predominantly duple or triple meter with the odd bit here or there. Certainly more possibilities exist if you slow down the tempo and start playing sixteenth-note figures. Check out Dream Theater, the Dave Holland Quintet, Tool, Liquid Tension Experiment, Bill Bruford, Brand X, Alan Holdsworth, Oz Noy, Scott Henderson, Frank Zappa, and the Mahavishnu Orchestra—all artists that perform intricate music with a high level of rhythmic complexity.

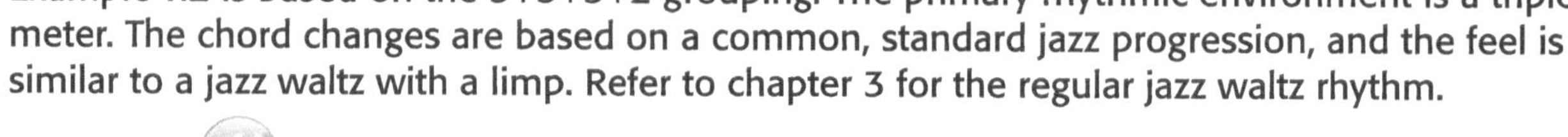

Example 7.2 is based on the 3+3+3+2 grouping. The primary rhythmic environment is a triple meter. The chord changes are based on a common, standard jazz progression, and the feel is similar to a jazz waltz with a limp. Refer to chapter 3 for the regular jazz waltz rhythm.

Example 7.2 Track 35

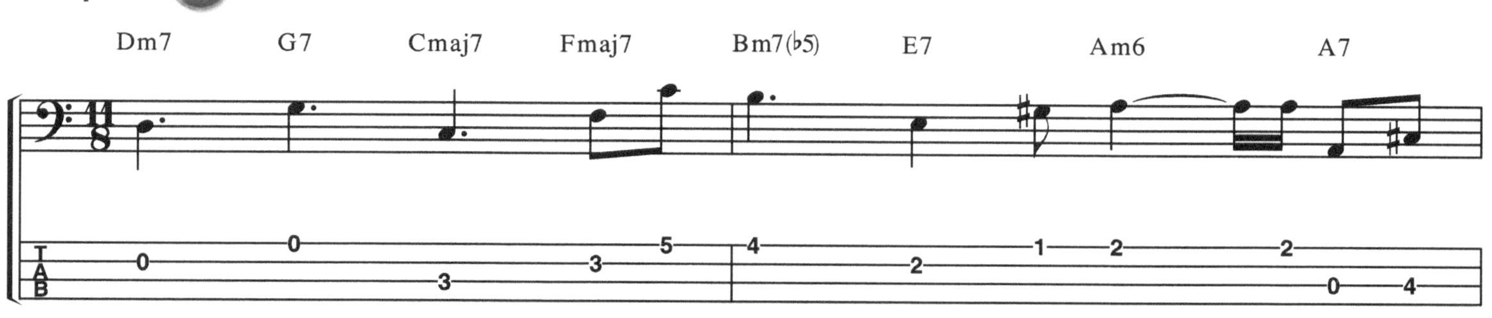

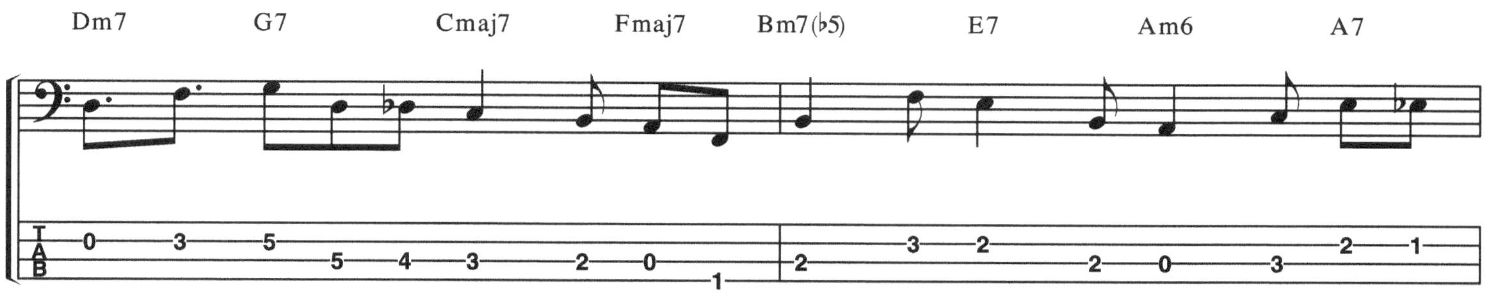

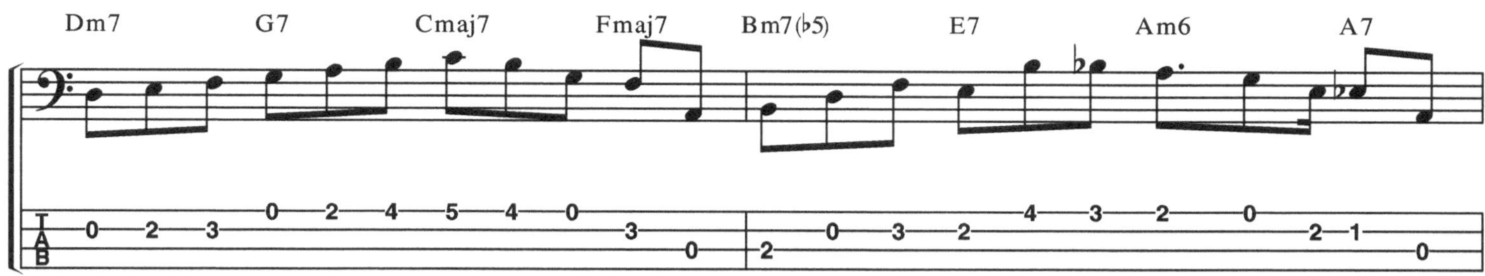

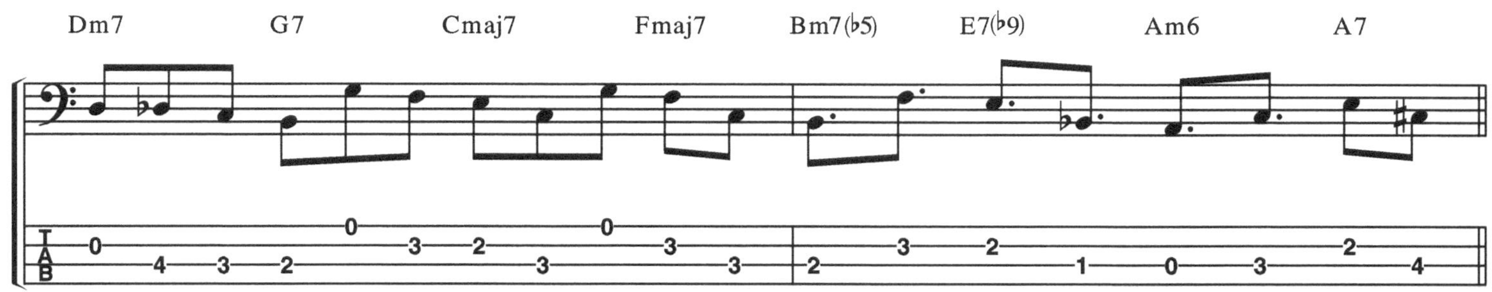

Example 7.3 is also a triple meter, but I've moved the group of two forward in the measure by three beats. The bass line is written from a 3+3+2+3 subdivision. The harmony is based on an 8-bar Chicago-style blues in A, and it feels like a stumbling shuffle danced with one shoe off. Those groupings of 3+3+2+3 indicate where the accents occur in the bass line. For maximum rhythmic power, you'd have the snare play a backbeat on the second and fourth groupings, i.e., beats 4 and 7.

Example 7.3  Track 36

Medium shuffle

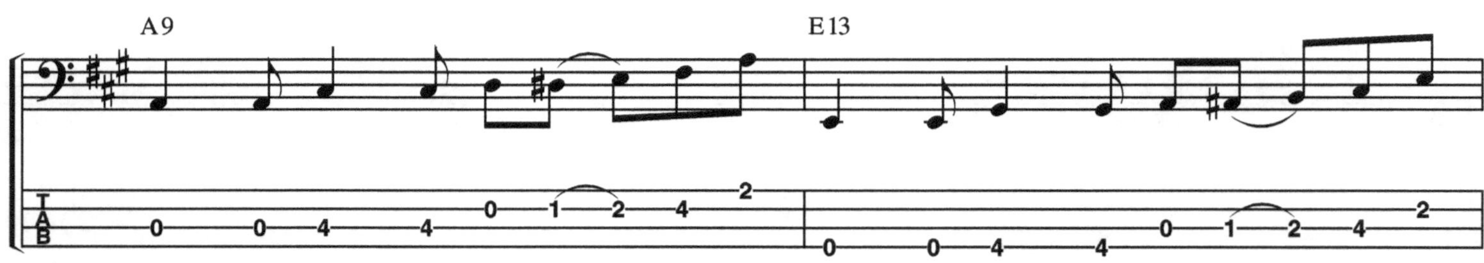

Comic relief moment: Have you heard the joke about the Greek drummer? The bandleader at a Greek wedding turns to the drummer and says "Hey, Spiro, this is a dance gig. Quit experimenting back there. Just keep the backbeat on 5 and 9, okay?"

In example 7.4, we return to the 3+3+3+2 subdivision, but now we're going to swing the sixteenth notes and get a triplet feel underneath each of the basic 3+3+3 groupings. Hip-hop and slow half-time funk shuffles use this rhythmic feel. The chords are based on an 8-bar jazz blues form. The rhythmic implication is of a modified $\frac{12}{8}$ feel.

Example 7.4  Track 37

Quasi jazz-waltz feel

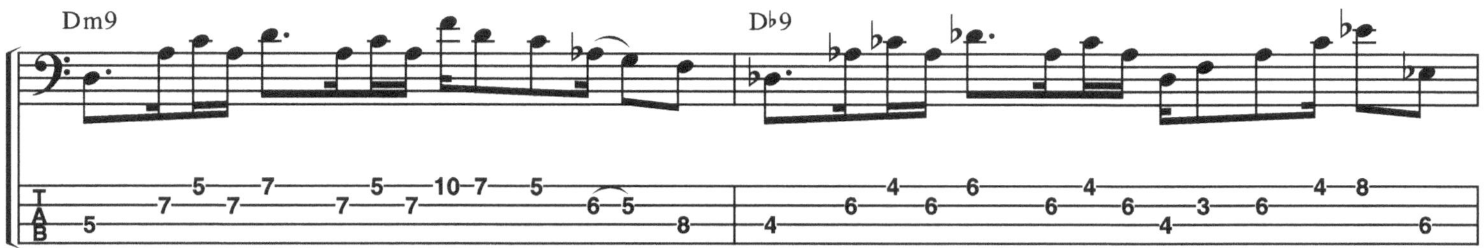

Example 7.5 is based on the 2+2+2+2+3 subdivision, a basic duple meter plus an extra odd group of three. The feel is straight eighth-note rock. The harmony is a static A7(♯9) vamp throughout. Notice that sometimes the bass line will lead in to the next bar with two dotted rhythms, which have a slightly hesitating rhythmic impetus. The other fills will be based on playing all three eighth notes. These have a more driving rhythmic quality that will create forward momentum and propel the bass line. The most aggressive fills are those based on sixteenth notes as in measures 2, 6, and 8. Use variations of these rhythmic effects to underscore the lyrics and melody of the song when you compose your own bass lines.

Example 7.5 Track 38

Example 7.6 also uses the 2+2+2+2+3 grouping, but with a faster tempo and a funkier style. In this feel, and at this tempo, more of the fills in the group of three should be based on sixteenth notes. This will be more rhythmically driving than three even eighth notes. We have six sixteenth notes in that group of three notes to rhythmically recombine.

For the fills, we have four options in this example. Three even eighths are used at the end of the first measure. In measure 2, the fill is in sixteenth notes slurred 2+2+2, which is simply a doubling of the even eighth-note rhythm in measure 1. In measure 4, the sixteenths are grouped 1+2+2+1, creating a syncopated lick. The last fill in measure 8 is an elaboration of two dotted eighth groups slurred as 2+1+2+1. There are, of course, many more options. Experiment with any one lick as the "groove unit," and use rhythmically contrasting groupings for your fills.

Example 7.6 Track 39

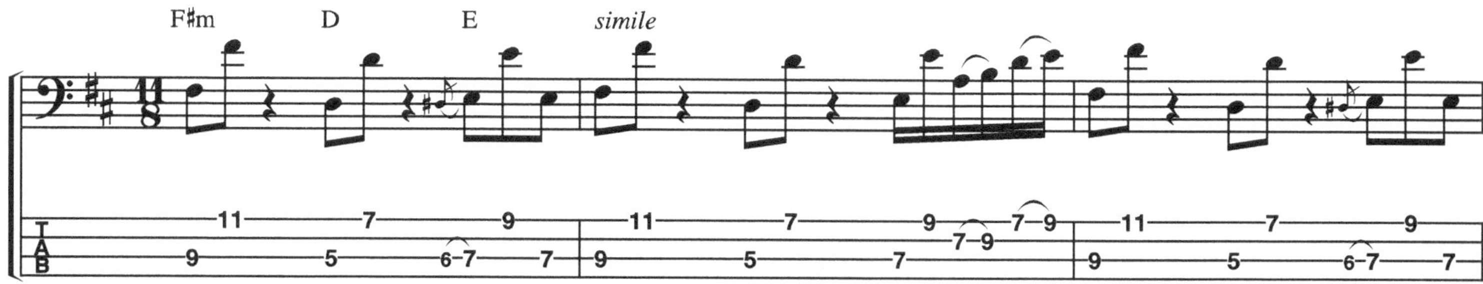

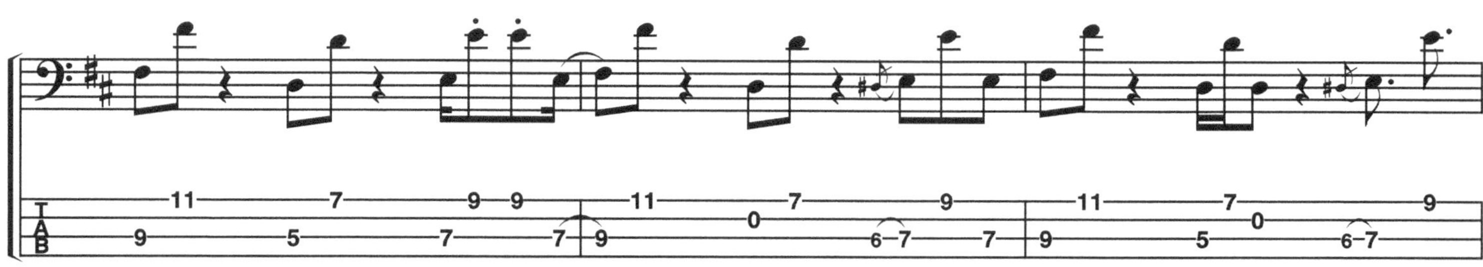

Example 7.7 is another duple-meter feel. Let's apply the groupings from examples 7.1.7 and 7.1.9 through 7.1.11. What we'll do is create a four-measure phrase with the odd group of three placed earlier in the phrase in each successive measure. I'll start with 7.1.5. Observe that we will maintain the dotted eighth subdivision of the group of three. Notice how moving the odd bit around in the phrase changes the rhythmic impact of the bass line.

Example 7.7 Track 40

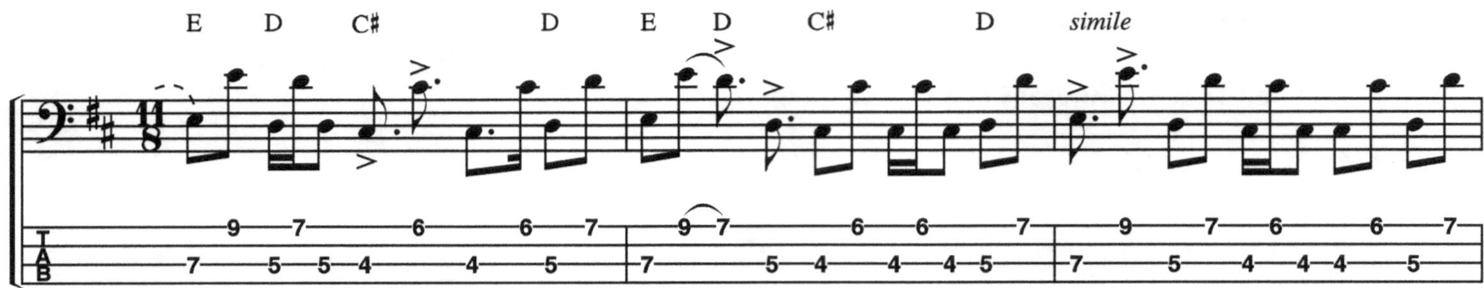

The groupings in the first four-measure phrase are 2+2+3+2+2 in the first measure, 2+3+2+2+2 in the second measure, 3+2+2+2+2 in the third measure, and back to our favorite 2+2+2+2+3 in the fourth measure. This alignment of the group of three is repeated in measures 5–8. Playing the odd group in different places in the phrase changes the drive of the bass figure. You can exploit these hesitating or driving qualities when you create your own bass lines.

Try selecting one grouping as the main groove unit and playing some, or all, of the other possible rhythms for fill licks, say, every four measures.

In practice, you might not always play a fill on the fourth measure, because drummers often do this to set up the next phrase. Your fill could, and should, echo or underscore a vocal or instrumental gesture. One bravura bass fill in the right place implies taste and maturity in your playing. I have found that frequent pointless licks contravene the function of the bass and annoy the listeners and the bandleader, your boss. Don't obscure the melody. You're in the **rhythm** section.

Use the worksheet concept to practice composing and playing bass lines in this meter. By now, you have seen the most common odd-meter rhythms, and you're well versed in the subdivision concept. Once you've bested the "elf" ("eleven" auf Deutsch), go on to the next chapter and we'll look at more arcane odd-meter rhythms.

Chapter 8

Really Odd: Groups of 13, 15, and More

In this chapter, we'll look at some really odd meters. We'll deal with large asymmetrical additive metric groupings and notation in sixteenth notes. You will find that these complex meters can be unraveled using the same small one-, two-, or three-note groupings we worked with in other odd meters. By the time you're done with this chapter, playing in $\frac{7}{4}$ will seem like child's play!

> *BWAH-HA-HA-HA-HA! (SFX: Evil laughter with deep reverb.)*

Seriously, the most complex rhythms can be deciphered using the even and odd subdivision approach. Any music that needs to be notated this way is usually instrumental and often features a dense rhythmic texture and lots of rapid ensemble figures. A textbook case would be the John McLaughlin composition "Birds of Fire" as performed by the Mahavishnu Orchestra.

"Birds of Fire" is notated in $\frac{18}{8}$ with a molto presto eighth note = 384 bpm! The guitar and keyboard melody lines are ripping through arpeggios and scalar licks in groups of 5 (2+3) +5 (2+3) +5 (2+3) +3. The bass and violin play the basic accompaniment riff in octaves, rhythmically grouped 3+3+2 plus 3+3+2+2 in each $\frac{18}{8}$ measure. They play a dotted quarter-note rhythm figure for the groups of three and both eighths in the groups of two.

If you look at the rhythm as 3+3+2 plus 3+3+2+2, it's easy to see that there's simply an extra two-beat grouping following a very common rhythm figure. Every folk guitarist on the planet plays that 3+3+2 rhythmic strumming pattern. Just for variety the drum pattern is organized around three even groups of six with snare hits on each group of six.

The music of India, which inspires John McLaughlin's fusion style, is also rhythmically and melodically complex. Indian music and Western music have radically different approaches to harmony. Indian classical music doesn't have chords as we know them in European music. In Indian music, harmony is the least exploited of the three fundamental aspects of musical art; rhythm and melody are primary.

What is known to musicologists as the *triputa ta'la*, a unit of rhythmic organization in South Indian music, could have a $\frac{7}{8}$ time signature, same as a Dream Theater song. The Dream Theater song will probably use chord structures of some kind, while a drone of one or two tones might provide the harmonic background for a performance of an Indian raga.

If we bassists are not playing an ensemble figure, then we'll be required to create a melodic line that supports some sort of harmony. We play the lowest-pitched melody in a band. Those bass melodies will require that bassists play lots of root tones with many reoccurring rhythmic phrases. If you dislike those musical guidelines, then you might consider playing some other instrument.

Later on in this chapter, we'll apply the rhythms to scales and chords. We can create some bass lines after we work out the rhythms themselves. By now, you're familiar with the magic dotted rhythms and the Three Steps to Mastery. Now, more than ever, it is necessary to tap the groupings on your body to internalize the rhythm. If you can feel the basic pulse in sixteenth notes, then you can group twos and threes at will.

Example 8.1. "BIRDS OF FIRE"

Birds of Fire

We'll begin our work in this chapter by taking an odd-meter figure from a previous chapter and putting it into sixteenth-note rhythms. Then we can add and/or subtract notes to create really wacky groupings. We will also experiment with organizing the groupings as a primarily "two" or primarily "three" feel with an odd bit interspersed. I'm going to cover 13 and 15 in this chapter, but the concepts would be the same in, say, $\frac{19}{16}$. Beware of an overly large number of beats. That many notes might be better notated in a mixed meter. We will cover mixed meters such as $\frac{7}{8} + \frac{4}{4}$ in chapter nine.

In example 8.2.1, we see a $\frac{7}{8}$ meter grouped 2+2+3. Example 8.2.2 shows the sixteenth-note groupings of that meter. Example 8.2.3 represents the longer-value quarter and dotted eighth rhythms that would be used in the bass line. We wrote a bass line for this rhythm in chapter 5. If we put $\frac{7}{8}$ into sixteenths, we would notate it as $\frac{14}{16}$. Now, if we subtract one sixteenth note, we'll be in $\frac{13}{16}$, definitely an "odd" meter!

Example 8.2

In example 8.3.1, we have $\frac{13}{16}$ grouped as 4+4+3+2. This subdivision feels like $\frac{2}{4} + \frac{5}{8}$. In example 8.3.2, we can reduce the two sixteenth-note groups down to eighth notes with one stray odd sixteenth somewhere in the figure. With this subdivision, we create a basic "two" feel with the odd sixteenth leading into the last eighth note. This rhythmic figure creates a skipping syncopation within what basically feels like a straight-eighth rock groove. Example 8.3.3 is the quarter-, dotted eighth-, eighth-note rhythm reduced from the groupings in example 8.3.2. We will write a bass line with this core rhythmic theme and two variations.

Example 8.3

Example 8.4 shows how this same meter, $\frac{13}{16}$, looks and feels when interpreted as a "three" feel plus some odd bits. Example 8.4.1 is grouped 3+3+3+2+2. Example 8.4.2 is the reduced rhythm that would make a strong definitive bass figure. The two eighth notes at the end of the measure set up the downbeat of the "three" feel by cascading forward into the next measure. Example 8.4.3 shows a contrasting pattern of 2+3+2+3+3 that would make a great fill figure as a variation to the basic groove rhythm of example 8.4.2.

Example 8.4

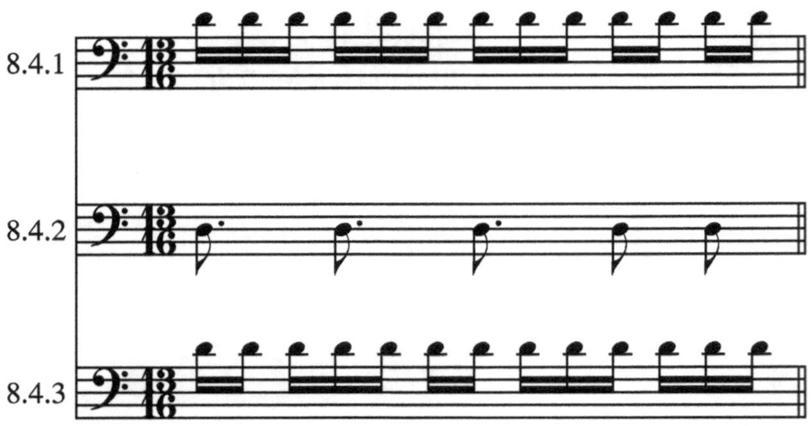

In example 8.5, we'll create a bass line using the rhythms from example 8.3. The rhythmic figure in 8.3.3 will be our basic groove unit (motif A). The first variation is in the second measure of the bass line (motif B), and is based on the rhythm of example 8.3.2. The second variation (motif C) is seen in the fourth measure of the phrase. Notice that motif C is based around a contrasting subdivision of 2+2+3+3+3. Measures 5–8 each feature a different grouping of twos and threes as sample variations.

The harmonic environment is bluesy E minor pentatonic. This style of rock music often uses power chords with no thirds, notated in example 8.5 as E5, and usually features lots of ensemble riffing. Meters such as $\frac{13}{16}$ afford the opportunity to write lots of fun odd accents in tutti passages. The bass would typically double the guitar, down an octave.

Example 8.5 Track 41

One more reminder about bass line composition: you only need four one-measure melodic phrases to create a developmental eight-measure bass line (A-B-A-C-A-B-A-D). The theme-and-variations compositional concept is centuries old and used in all styles of popular music. It may seems contrived to think of bass-line construction this way, but the contrast of repetition and variation, security and anxiety, is what people like to hear in a bass line. Repetition in the bass line is important in odd meter performance. Rick Laird's bass lines were the "glue" in the Mahavishnu Orchestra performances.

In example 8.6, we have the realization of the primarily "three" feel notated in example 8.4. The harmonic milieu is bluesy E minor pentatonic. The basic groove unit rhythm is from example 8.4.3. The fill in the fourth measure is based on the contrasting 2+3+2+3+3 subdivision shown in example 8.4.2. Notice that the variations used in measures 2, 4, and 6 are melodic, not rhythmic.

Example 8.6 Track 42

In example 8.7, we add one beat to the original $\frac{14}{16}$ notation of $\frac{7}{8}$ from example 8.2 and create the meter $\frac{15}{16}$. Example 8.7.1 shows $\frac{15}{16}$ grouped 4+4+4+3. This subdivision feels like sixteenth-note rock with a stumble forward. Example 8.7.2 is one possible way to group the eighth notes plus the one sixteenth. Example 8.7.3 is a good bass line rhythm motif, based on example 8.7.2, that has been reduced to quarter-note rhythmic density. Notice that the group of three sixteenth notes has been moved up in the phrase (4+4+3+4).

Example 8.7

In example 8.8, let's apply the rhythm of example 8.7.3 to a 12-bar rock blues. This form will be best written as a six-measure form when notated in $\frac{15}{16}$. The longer rhythmic unit of $\frac{15}{16}$ will result in a sort of spastic version of a sixteenth-note rock beat. This example feels primarily like a $\frac{4}{4}$ bar with a skip. Notice the use of three dotted eighths for the setup fill in the fourth measure of the bass line.

Example 8.8  Track 43

Now let's look at $\frac{15}{16}$ interpreted as a "three" feel, with groups of three sixteenths as our basic accent grouping. This subdivision will feel like a five with a triplet pulse. In example 8.9.1, we see five groups of sixteenths (3+3+3+3+3). Each group of three receives a primary accent. Example 8.9.2 shows a rhythmically contrasting subdivision (2+3+2+3+2+3) that would make a nifty fill figure. Example 8.9.3 shows a larger rhythmic subdivision that could be used in a bass line.

Example 8.9

Let's apply this rhythm to a blues song form to create what will feel like a "shuffle in five." In adapting a 12-bar blues for example 8.10, as in example 8.8, I opted to shorten the harmonic form and write a six-measure cycle. Notice in this example that in the last grouping of each measure, all three sixteenth notes are played as a setup fill into the next measure.

Example 8.10  Track 44

When you write in meters such as $\frac{15}{16}$, you'll want to exploit all the possibilities available to create interesting asymmetrical accents by mixing groups of two and three. As we have seen in examples 8.5, 8.8, and 8.10, a rhythmic grouping that contrasts with the basic "two" or "three" feel makes a great fill rhythm. Drummers use this approach all the time. Let's mix groupings of twos and threes and create a bass line from the rhythm we create.

In example 8.11.1, we see $\frac{15}{16}$ grouped as 3+3+3+2+2+2. Example 8.11.2 is a contrasting figure based around three consecutive 3+2 groupings. This is the retrograde of the rhythm in example 8.9.2. Example 8.11.3 is a suggested bass line rhythm. The syncopated figure in example 8.11.4 would make a great fill rhythm.

Example 8.11

Example 8.12, based on the rhythm of example 8.11.1, is an adaptation of the blues form seen in example 8.10. Mixing the groups of three and two creates more rhythmic interest. This bass line sounds more like a rock blues than a shuffle in five. The contrasting rhythm from example 8.11.2 (3+2+3+2+3+2) is used in measure 4 as a fill rhythm. The retrograde rhythm (2+3+2+3+2+3) seen in example 8.9.2 is used for a turnaround lick in the last measure.

Example 8.12 Track 45

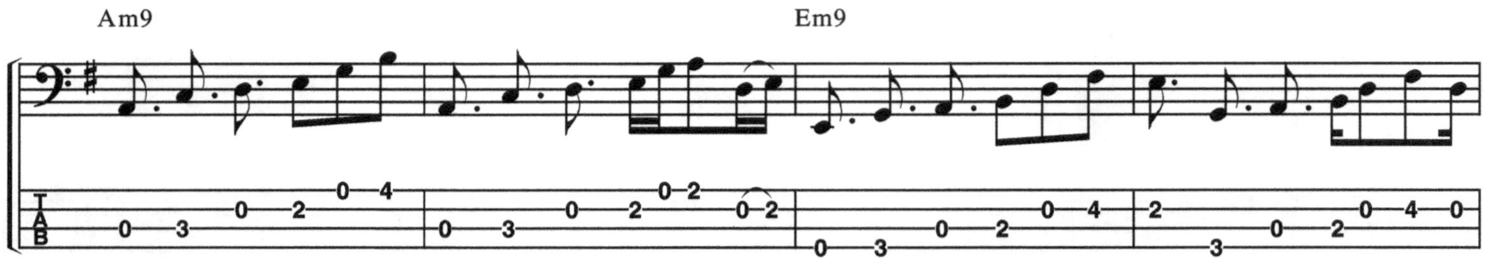

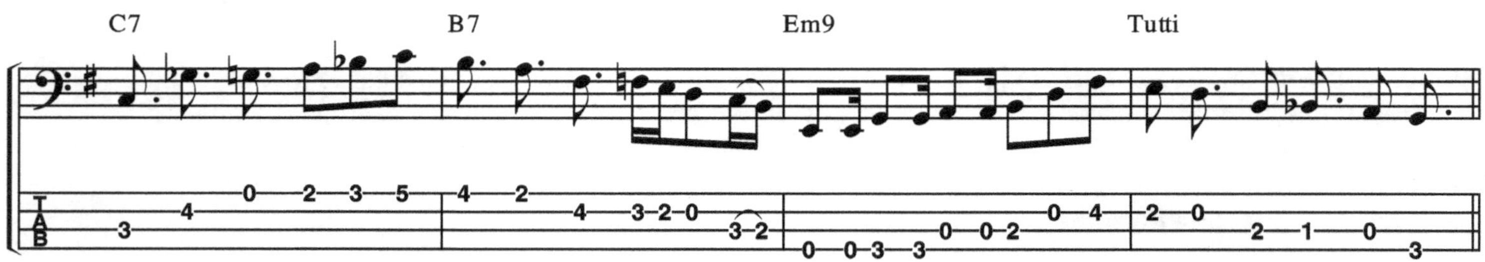

So now you know everything about odd meters, or at least you have a working procedure to unravel even the most intricate rhythmic puzzles. Create your own worksheets to practice $\frac{13}{16}$ and $\frac{15}{16}$. Obviously, there are other complex meters to play. I encourage you to experiment when you practice.

You could pick any lick in $\frac{4}{4}$ and try adding a sixteenth note somewhere in the phrase and play in $\frac{17}{16}$. Or, you might take an odd meter such as $\frac{5}{4}$, think in sixteenth notes ($\frac{20}{16}$), and drop a note to create $\frac{19}{16}$. You could use these as symmetrical rhythms for fills in the basic feel, or as the groove unit itself.

Write out some subdivision ideas for improvising. Seeing the figures on paper where you can manipulate them with a pencil and eraser is very liberating and enlightening. Once you're comfortable in sixteenth-based odd meters, go to chapter 9 to investigate mixed-meter compositions, soloing in odd meters, and using odd-meter concepts in common time signatures to create unusual rhythmic phrases.

Chapter 9

Mixed-Meter Music

In this chapter, we're going to combine the different meters we have covered thus far. We'll do some work with mixed-meter compositions and playing odd-meter phrases over the bar line against $\frac{4}{4}$. We will learn how to manipulate the levels of chordal, scalar, and chromatic notes to create interesting bass melodies and solos in odd meters.

Let's quickly review a few important concepts. In the first three chapters, we learned the techniques needed to work with any time signature, odd or even. Here are five essential working procedures:

1. Think in subdivision groups to reduce complex rhythms into manageable parts.

2. Use the Three Steps to Mastery method to solve rhythmic and harmonic problems.

3. Compose a bass line using the theme-and-variations concept.

4. Conceive of the level of harmonic density you're using in your bass line.

5   Play rhythmic and/or melodically unique fill figures at ends of phrases.

To have fun with odd meters, you don't have to be just in an odd meter. For example, interesting odd-meter ensemble passages could alternate with "normal" grooves. Check out "Time to Kill" by the British art-rock band U.K. The verse phrases are nine beats long, alternating between $\frac{4}{4}$ and $\frac{5}{4}$. The bridge of a song could be in another meter than the verse section. In "Money" by Pink Floyd, the verse is a seven-beat phrase grouped 4+3 that transitions into a minor blues jam in a $\frac{4}{4}$ shuffle. The verses to "All You Need Is Love" by the Beatles are notated in alternating measures of $\frac{4}{4}$ and $\frac{3}{4}$ and the choruses are in $\frac{4}{4}$.

Ensemble riffs, intros, and endings are instrumental sections of tunes that could use the odd-meter or polyrhythmic treatment. Instrumental interludes could be in, say, $\frac{7}{8}$ phrases over $\frac{4}{4}$ in the drums. The accents in the melody will be displaced against the drum pattern at the top of each melodic cycle. "Kashmir," by Led Zeppelin, is based on a slow three-beat phrase cycling against a simple $\frac{4}{4}$ straight eighth-note rock beat.

Mixed-meter music refers to compositions that contain at least two different metric groupings. This could even include any tune in $\frac{4}{4}$ that has a $\frac{2}{4}$ measure to extend or shorten a phrase; however, the idea of mixed meters implies a more extensive use of measures with different denominators. What I see most commonly is the use of odd-meter or unusual rhythmic phrases to delineate different sections of the composition. The verse of a song could be in $\frac{6}{4}$ while the chorus might "straighten out" and go to $\frac{4}{4}$.

 "The Crunge," by Led Zeppelin, is a good example of a mixed-meter funk tune. You could write the rhythm out in $\frac{9}{8}$, but it basically feels like a measure of $\frac{3}{4}$ followed by a measure of $\frac{3}{8}$. The band Dream Theater uses mixed meters extensively. For example, they might play a passage of 12 measures in $\frac{5}{4}$ followed by a repeated lick in $\frac{9}{16}$, then another repeated riff in $\frac{11}{16}$. The odd-meter sections are repeated to reinforce them to the listener. For an extreme example of this concept, check out music by the band Meshuggah.

Let's start our work with thinking in subdivisions. Example 9.1 demonstrates the simple division of groups of three eighth or sixteenth notes. The two possible combinations are 1+2 or 2+1. We could use these three-beat rhythmic cells to create interesting syncopated patterns against a basic $\frac{4}{4}$ beat pattern. I chose easy-to-finger notes to use with the various rhythms.

Example 9.1

9.1.1

9.1.2

9.1.3

9.1.4

9.1.5

9.1.6

In example 9.1.1, we're in $\frac{7}{4}$, so we need four 1+2 groups and one group of 2 to complete a measure. The first measure is grouped 1+2 (x4) +2. The second measure shows the retrograde rhythm of 2+1 (x4) +2. The accent patterns of the two measures are opposites.

Example 9.1.2 is in $\frac{9}{4}$, a meter that is divisible by three, so we have six 1+2 or 2+1 groupings available. The first measure is the 1+2 subdivision and the second measure shows the 2+1 grouping.

Example 9.1.3 demonstrates this concept in the familiar $\frac{12}{8}$ meter. The first measure has the 1+2 group. The second measure is the shuffle rhythm created by the 2+1 group.

Example 9.1.4 is the same 1+2 concept applied to $\frac{4}{4}$, a meter that is not evenly divisible by three. Now we get five groups of three and the odd one. I grouped the last 3+1 as 2+2 to create a common $\frac{4}{4}$ rock bass line. The second measure is based on the retrograde rhythmic grouping of 2+1.

Example 9.1.5 is the same melodic phrase as seen in example 9.1.4, except it is written in sixteenth notes. The second measure of this example is the same melodic pattern altered to fit a $\frac{9}{8}$ meter grouped 3+3+3+2. Example 9.1.6 shows the bass line adapted to $\frac{11}{8}$ (3+3+3+2), and the second measure shows the pattern extrapolated to $\frac{13}{8}$ (3+3+3+2+2). Recombining the thousands of possible groupings will create some startling rhythmic effects in your bass lines and solos.

Example 9.2 is a mixed-meter song form with a set of chord changes. This will be our mixed meter rhythmic and harmonic template from which we will compose our bass line. I have chosen subdivisions of each measure that will be the rhythmic foundation of my bass line.

Example 9.2

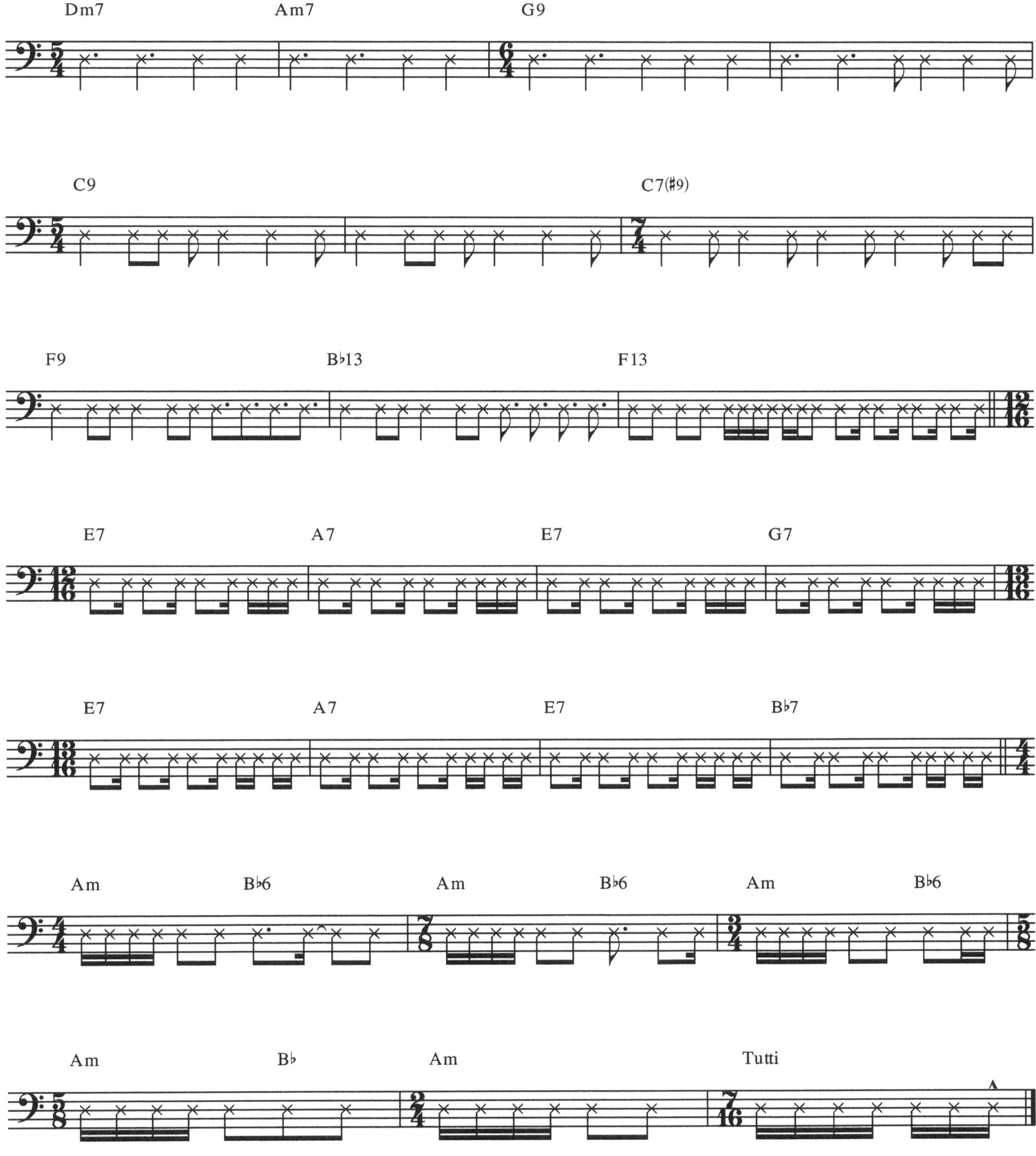

Example 9.3 is a bass line realization of the rhythms and chord changes in example 9.2. I have written this bass line at the first level of harmonic density, meaning chord tones only up to a seventh-chord level of harmonic density. There are no scalar or chromatic tones used in this example.

Example 9.3 Track 46

Example 9.4 illustrates a scalar approach to the template of example 9.2. This example is written at the second level of harmonic density. The bass line employs chordal and scalar tones, but no chromatic notes.

Example 9.4  Track 47

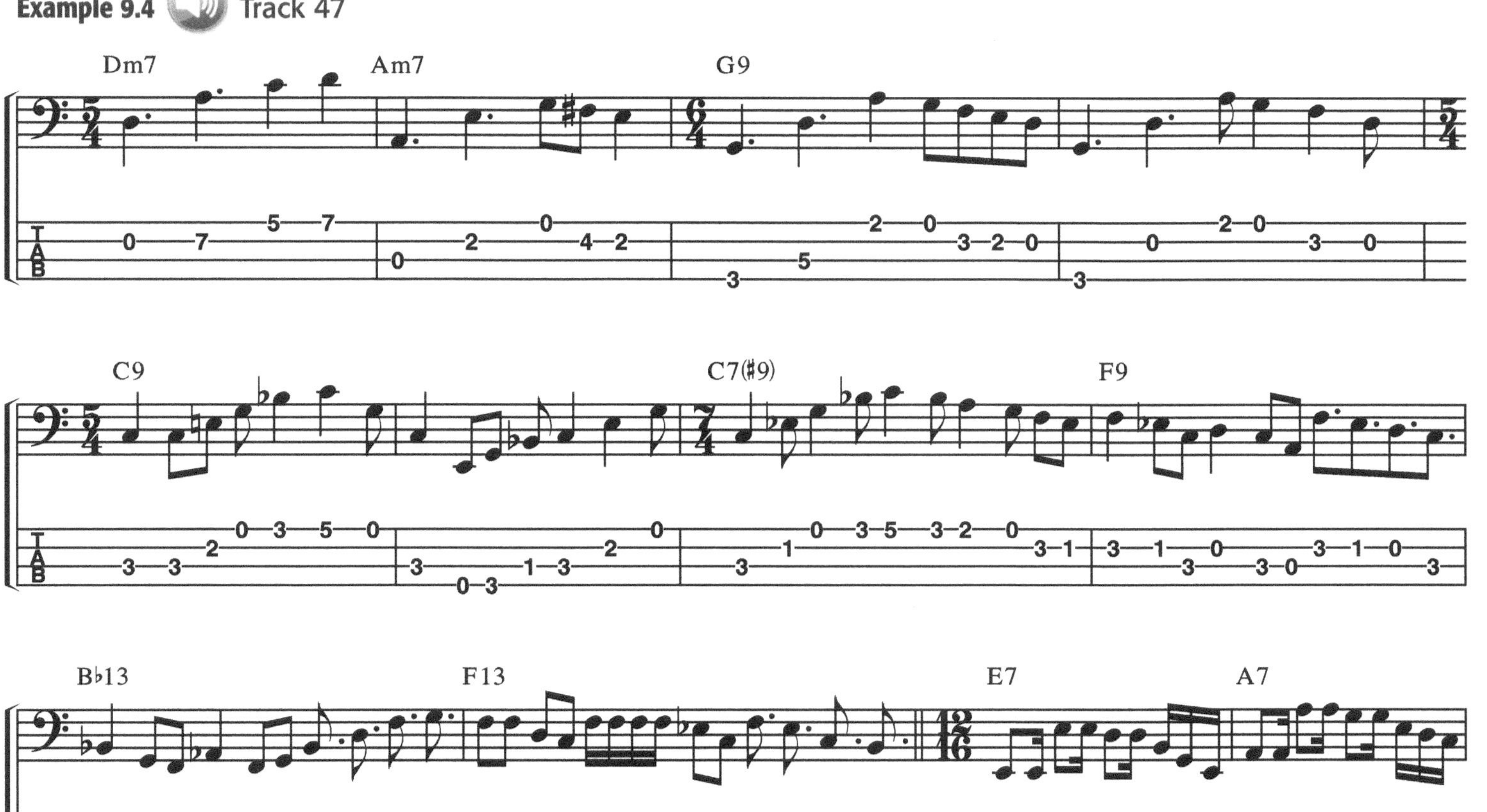

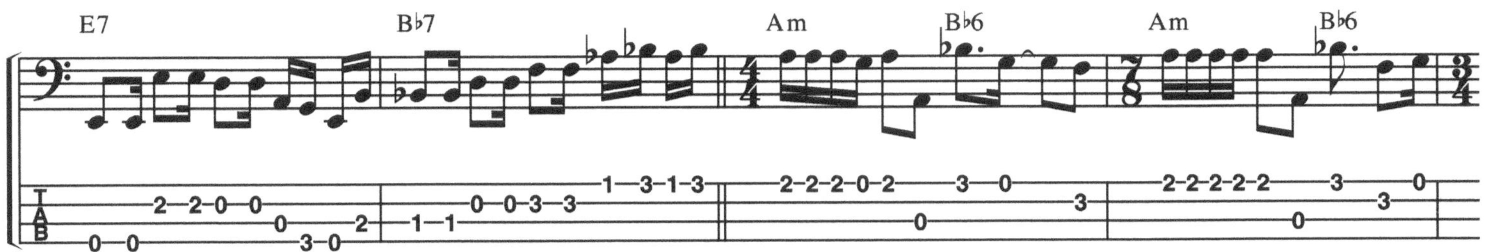

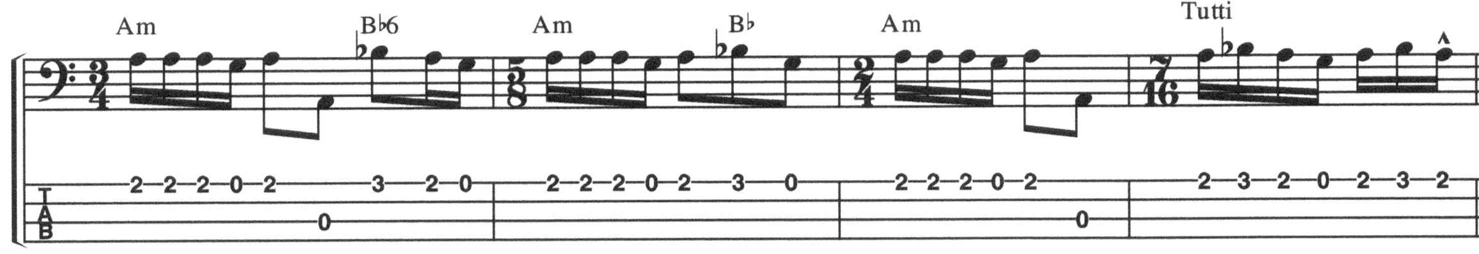

Example 9.5 is also based on the template of example 9.2. Here, the bass line is written at the third, or chromatic, level of harmonic density; however, as in any well-constructed, functional bass line, it is comprised predominantly of chord tones to support the harmony. The scale and chromatic tones are used to add melodic interest to the line and lead the ear into the next section of the piece, most frequently at the end of a phrase.

Example 9.5 Track 48

I've only written one mixed-meter example, because there is no common mixed-meter song form. The idea here is to develop a working procedure for problem solving, not practice some arbitrary example I made up. You should try to compose your own pieces using the proven effective techniques detailed in this book. That is the path to mastery of odd meters—play them!

Before we close this chapter, we need to discuss how to create the rhythmic effect of an odd meter in an even meter. We can play rhythmic figures that are grouped over the bar line to produce uncommon phrasing. One technique would be to take odd groupings and superimpose them against an even-meter drum pattern. This will create accents in unusual places within a standard four-measure phrase in a common meter such as $\frac{4}{4}$. Example 9.6 shows one possible phrase created with this technique. The first four measures are a common i-iv-V chord progression in A minor. This phrase sounds like something you'd hear on any reggae recording. By extending the bass line phrases from four to five beats, we can create an interesting variation on the basic phrase.

Measures 5 to 12 of example 9.6 show the result of this alteration of the bass line. Notice that the new melodic phrase is built from melodic cells in a 5+5+4+2 grouping of quarter notes. The total number of beats is 16 quarter notes—still a basic four-measure phrase in $\frac{4}{4}$. This odd melodic phrasing creates a bass line that sounds familiar, yet unusual, as a result of the offset by one beat from what would be expected in a standard reggae bass figure.

By stating the roots of the chords later than expected, the bass line also moves the harmonic rhythm. I now will play the chords offset as well. The harmonic rhythm is now grouped as 6+6+4 (=16). The E chord is now only played for one measure at the end of the phrase. We have given this cliché i-iv-V chord progression in A minor a fresh treatment solely by manipulating the rhythmic aspect of the music.

Example 9.6 Track 49

Of course, this is one of thousands of possibilities. Your assignment, should you accept it, is to use what you've learned to create your own unique musical statement. You now have the tools at your disposal to master rhythm in any manifestation, odd or even.

When first introduced to these principles, I had a hard time with odd meters and syncopation. The application of the techniques shown in this book helped me, and I guarantee that they will help you solve any rhythmic problem you encounter. I hope that you will explore odd-meter rhythms, and that the work *you* do on the journey will spark your creativity.

Chapter 10

The Songs (Basically Remain the Same)

The title of this chapter is a tip of the hat to Led Zeppelin, one of the truly great rock bands. They combined the earthy energy of American blues, the lyrical pseudo-mysticism of British art rock, and innovative use of odd meters to reshape the conventions of rock music. They managed to be basic and sophisticated at the same time.

This chapter is not about Led Zeppelin's music. It is all about *you* applying what we've covered in this book. What we'll do in this chapter is take a song form that is commonly in $\frac{4}{4}$ meter and do versions in some of the various odd meters we have studied. By having a benchmark compositional form, we'll have a basis to compare and appreciate the rhythmic effects created by each odd meter.

After much thought, I've chosen various forms of blues tunes to use. Blues music has influenced almost every aspect of American popular music in the last 50 years. The performance practices of blues artists have profoundly influenced the singing and playing mannerisms of contemporary artists. The unique melodic and harmonic structure of the blues also survives unadulterated today. A modern blues recording or performance will contain the same basic stylistic elements used in the post-World War II electric blues of seminal musicians such as Muddy Waters, B.B. King, Jimmy Reed, and Willie Dixon.

I have used the blues form in previous chapters, but in different keys and styles. In this chapter, we'll stay in the same key and create various treatments of the same basic song. Each example will use either a 12-bar or 8-bar blues harmonic form. I based the length of the form on what felt right in each meter. For melodic and harmonic variety, I've written an example in the minor mode. Tempos will differ from meter to meter as best suits the feel of whatever specific odd time signature we're using.

I want to exploit the familiarity of the blues form to contrast with whatever odd meter we're working on. The characteristic use of dominant 7th harmony, the use of "blue notes" that lend a minor quality to major-mode blues, and the triplet-based shuffle rhythm are characteristic in the canon of the blues. These elements are all used in the examples in this chapter. We're only going to alter the metric unit used to organize these familiar blues phrases.

Example 10.1 is a basic 12-bar blues in a major tonality. The definitive harmonic structure is indicated in upper-case Roman numerals next to the chord symbols. A good example of this form is "How Many More Years" by Howlin' Wolf.

Example 10.1

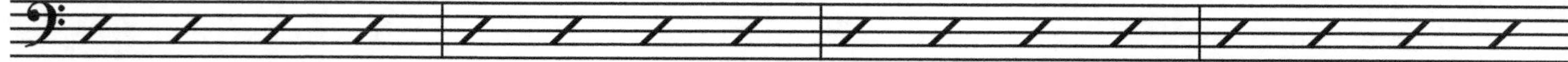

Example 10.2 is a 12-bar blues in a minor mode, with minor chords notated in lower-case Roman numerals. Notice the alternate chords used in measures 9 and 10. This is common to minor blues. A good example of this form is "The Thrill Is Gone" by B.B. King.

Example 10.2

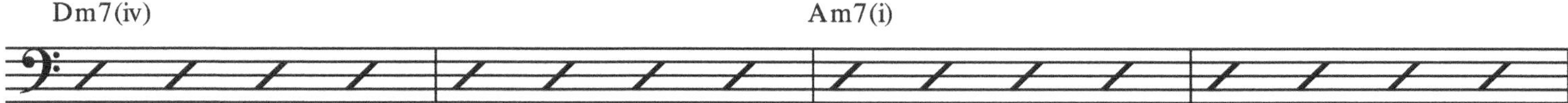

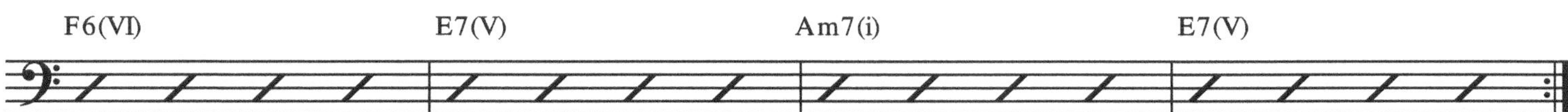

Example 10.3 is an 8-bar blues composition in a major mode. This harmonic progression is definitive of the form. A good example of the 8-bar blues is "Key to the Highway" by Big Bill Broonzy.

Example 10.3

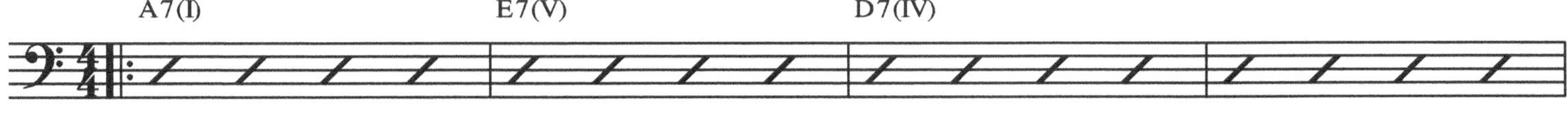

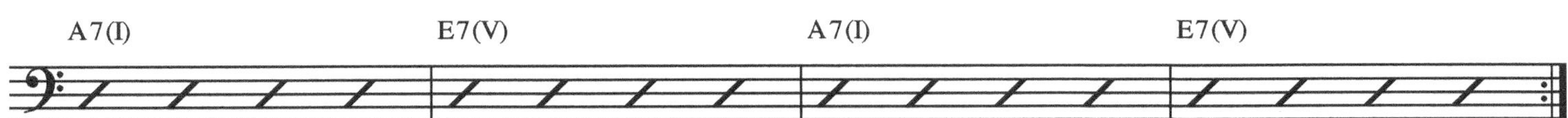

The preceding three simple variations of the blues will be the basis upon which we will work our rhythmic magic. I hope you'll enjoy the results. Use the audio tracks to practice bass lines and soloing. An effective way to study the various meters would be to repeat an audio track and alternate between playing a bass line and soloing over the song form.

Example 10.4 is a 12-bar minor blues in $\frac{5}{4}$. Measures 1 and 2 state the basic riff. Notice that measure 4 varies rhythmically and has a melodic fill into the vi chord (D minor) in measure 5. The turnaround in measures 9 and 10 uses the **VI** (F) to **V** (E7) cadence typical of minor blues. There is a unique rhythmic figure on both E7 chords to help define the turnaround at the end of the 12-bar form.

Example 10.4  Track 50

Example 10.5 is based on a 12-bar major blues form with a straight eighth-note rock/blues feel; however, the $\frac{7}{4}$ time signature really feels like two measures of $\frac{4}{4}$ minus a beat. When written in $\frac{7}{4}$, the result is this six-measure blues form. This eighth-note subdivision of $\frac{7}{4}$ is 2+2+2+2+3+3. Think $\frac{4}{4} + \frac{3}{4}$ with the last 3+3 eighth notes played as dotted quarters or quarter and eighth-note groups.

Example 10.5 🔊 Track 51

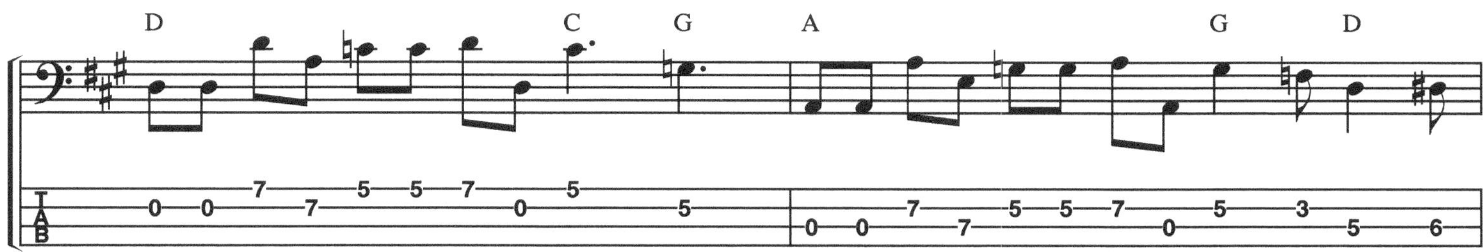

Example 10.6 is basically example 10.5 written in $\frac{7}{8}$. This example illustrates the difference in feel between a quarter-note rhythm and an eighth-note rhythm. The form is now half as long, and the tempo needs to be slower than example 10.5 or else it will feel frantic. You could transform this six-measure form into a 12-bar blues by repeating the basic two-measure bass figures in the appropriate measures.

Example 10.6 🔊 Track 52

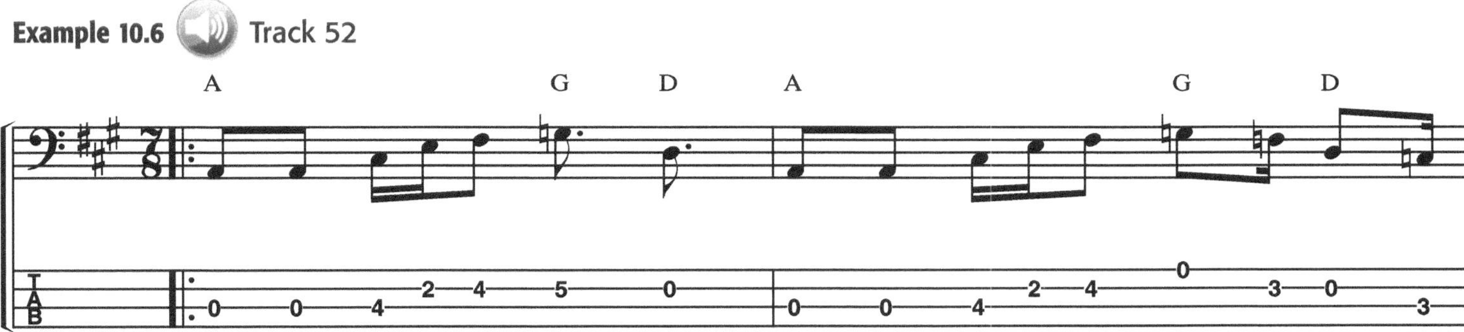

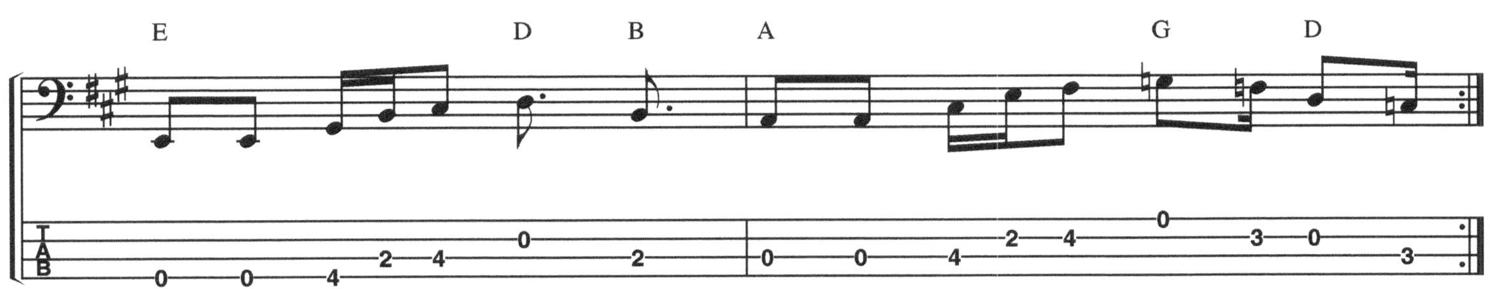

In example 10.7, the $\frac{9}{8}$ meter seems to lend itself to the 8-bar blues form. The basic riff in measure 1 is repeated with little variation in this example. Notice the fill figure at the end of measure 4, the octave displacement of the line in measure 6, and the truncated turnaround figure in measures 7 and 8. The feel is a shuffle with long-short 2+1 groupings of three eighth notes as the motor rhythm.

Example 10.7  Track 53

This last example is based on a common 12-bar blues shuffle. Now that we're in $\frac{11}{8}$, I'm going to feel a three-based rhythm with an odd "two" bit somewhere in each measure. Measures 1–3 are grouped 3+3+3+2. I vary the rhythm in the fourth measure to create a fill figure into the IV chord, D7. In measures 5 and 6, I move the two bit earlier in the figure, resulting in a 3+3+2+3 grouping.

In measures 7 and 8, we return to the basic 3+3+3+2 riff. In the last four-bar phrase, the two bit is played one group earlier in each measure. Measure 9 is 3+3+3+2, measure 10 is 3+3+2+3, measure 11 is 3+2+3+3, and measure 12 is 2+3+3+3.

Example 10.8 Track 54

Now that we have worked through a few examples of altering common song forms and rhythmic feels, it's up to you to find situations to use these new ideas. Employing these rhythmic techniques will make tired musical material seem fresh and different, yet still familiar and accessible to the listener. I guarantee that using odd-meter concepts in regular meters and with common song forms will stimulate your creativity. Now go forth and be odd.

Bibliography and Discography

It's ironic that this last section may be the first you should address. Listening to the music itself is the best teacher, so I have drawn up a very short list of examples to listen to and some books to investigate. Once you're familiar with the techniques introduced in chapters 1 through 3, any odd-meter music, in any style, will be much less mysterious. In chapters 4 through 9, we applied those techniques to hypothetical musical examples. I guarantee that the material in those chapters will reflect what you'll hear on these recordings.

There is also a list of bassists as a sample of names to look for if you want to hear players who excel in odd-meter performance and composition. I'm sure there are other great players out there and new ones coming up all the time. These bassists, and others, can be heard on the recordings in the suggested listening list.

A list of suggested composers, many from the "serious art music" world, is also included. Some of these are contemporary as of the writing of this book, and others were active before the turn of the 20th century. These composers purposefully use odd and/or mixed meters in their works. Check them out; you'll be surprised how "modern" their music sounds. Classical composers often introduce progressive ideas and techniques that find their way into popular music. Is it really coincidental that the opening measures of Béla Bartók's *String Quartet No. 5* (1934) sound like full-tilt Led Zeppelin?

Bibliography

Drummer's Guide to Odd Meters, Ed Roscetti. Musician's Institute Press, 2000.

Elementary Training for Musicians, Paul Hindemith. Schott Publishing, 1946.

Even in the Odds, Ralph Humphrey. C. L. Barnhouse, 1980.

Funkifying the Clave: Afro-Cuban Grooves for Bass and Drums, Lincoln Goines and Robby Ameen. Alfred Music, 1993.

Modern Reading Text in 4/4: For All Instruments, Louis Bellson written in collaboration with Gil Breines. Alfred Music, 1968.

Musician's Guide to Polyrhythms, Peter Magadini. Try Publishing, 1967.

Odd Meter Bassics, Dino Monoxelos. Musician's Institute Press, 1998.

Odd Time Reading Text: For All Instruments, Louis Bellson and Gil Breines. Alfred Music, 1968.

Suggested Listening

Apostrophe, Frank Zappa

The Best of Free Flight, Jim Walker and Freeflight

Birds of Fire, Mahavishnu Orchestra

Blue Rondo, Richard Greene

Dark Side of the Moon, Pink Floyd

Electric Bath, The Don Ellis Orchestra

Eternal Wind, Eternal Wind

Extensions, Dave Holland Quartet

Fat Albert Rotunda, Herbie Hancock

Fragile, Yes

Gradually Going Tornado, Bill Bruford

Houses of the Holy, Led Zeppelin

Led Zeppelin IV, Led Zeppelin

Modern Times, Steps Ahead

Texas Rumba, Harvie S.

Time Out, The Dave Brubeck Quartet

Shakti with John McLaughlin, Shakti with John McLaughlin

Recommended Artists

Aquarium Rescue Unit

Jeff Berlin and Vox Humana

Bill Bruford

Brand X

Coliseum

The Dave Brubeck Quartet

Dave Holland Quartet/Gateway Quartet

Devo

The Don Ellis Orchestra

Dream Theater

Eternal Wind

Genesis

Scott Henderson/TribalTech

Alan Holdsworth

King Crimson

Led Zeppelin

Liquid Tension Experiment

Mahavishnu Orchestra

Phish

Pink Floyd

Shakti with John McLaughlin

Tool

UK

Yes

Frank Zappa

Recommended Composers

Béla Bartók

Leonard Bernstein

Joseph Curiale

Milcho Leviev

Hank Levy

John Serry

Igor Stravinsky

L. Subramanian

Recommended Bassists

Jeff Andrews (Steps Ahead)

Victor Bailey (solo artist / Weather Report)

Jeff Berlin (solo artist / Bill Bruford / Alan Holdsworth)

Oteil Burbridge (Aquarium Rescue Unit)

Dave Carpenter (Alan Holdsworth)

Paul D'Amour (Tool)

Tom Fowler (Frank Zappa)

Eddie Gomez (Chick Corea / Steps Ahead)

Jimmy Haslip (Yellowjackets)

Dave Holland (solo artist / Gateway)

Todd Johnson (solo artist)

John Paul Jones (Led Zeppelin)

Abraham Laboriel (studio virtuoso)

Jim Lacefield (Freeflight)

Rick Laird (Mahavishnu Orchestra)

John Myung (Dream Theater)

David Parlato (The Don Ellis Orchestra)

Jaco Pastorius (solo artist / Weather Report)

John Pattitucci (solo artist / Chick Corea)

Harvie S. (solo artist)

Chris Squire (Yes)

Gary Willis (Tribal Tech)

Victor Wooten (solo artist / Béla Fleck and the Flecktones)

"Senator" Eugene Wright (The Dave Brubeck Quartet)

About the Author

Tim Emmons is an active freelance musician in the Los Angeles area and a veteran performer of over 125 film and television scores, including *Ratouille, The Simpsons, Family Guy, Mission Impossible III, The Incredibles, The Day After Tomorrow, Something's Gotta Give*, and *The Wedding Planner*. He has played in the pit and on stage for dozens of major theatrical productions, including *Too Old for the Chorus, Curtains, Swing, Candide, Swan Lake*, and *Ragtime*. Additionally, PC game players hear him on the soundtracks to *Fall of Liberty, Splinter Cell, Halo, Call of Duty*, and *Jumper*.

An eclectic musician, Tim has played contrabass for Stevie Wonder and Beyoncé, Josh Groban, Justin Timberlake, Kenny G., Andrea Boccelli, Brandy, John Tesh, and Toni Braxton. He has performed with a diverse array of artists, including jazz guitar virtuoso Joe Pass, blues pioneer Bo Diddley, master jazz saxophonist Art Pepper, swing-era legend Lionel Hampton, Broadway diva Liza Minelli, disco queen Donna Summer, Broadway icons Carol Channing and John Raitt, rock veteran Rod Stewart, and scat-singing innovator Cab Calloway.

In 2000, Tim joined Freeflight, the seminal classical-jazz-fusion ensemble founded in 1982 by former L.A. Philharmonic principal flautist Jim Walker. In 2001, he arranged, conducted, and performed music for the soundtrack of HBO's F. Scott Fitzgerald biopic, Last Call, and the Peter Bogdanovich indie gem The Cat's Meow. Tim also arranges for and directs actor Jeff Goldblum's Mildred Snitzer Orchestra. A busy educator, he teaches bass and directs the Jazz Ensemble at Occidental College in Los Angeles. He is also a bass instructor at California State University L.A., Azusa Pacific University, the University of Redlands, the University of California at Riverside, and Musician's Institute in Hollywood.